WORKS OF ART
IN THE HOUSE OF LORDS

Works of Art in the House of Lords

Edited by Maurice Bond

London
Her Majesty's Stationery Office

© Crown copyright 1980
First published 1980

ISBN 0 11 700897 4

Printed in England for Her Majesty's
Stationery Office by Ebenezer Baylis & Son Ltd,
The Trinity Press, Worcester.

Demand No 596480   K80

Design by HMSO Graphic Design/Dennis Greeno.

i *(Frontispiece)* Queen Victoria with Justice and
Mercy. *John Gibson, 1856, sculpture in marble, bas-
reliefs on pedestal. Statue of Queen Victoria, 8 feet
(2·44 m) high* INSCRIBED *'Queen Victoria 1837–1901
[and] J Gibson fecit Romae'. Walker, iii, 74–5.*

Contents

List of Figures

Note: The 'works of art' in the House of Lords referred to in the title and described in detail in the text are listed consecutively in the *List of Plates*. All other illustrative material in this book is shown in the following *List of Figures*. For abbreviations see p 10 below.

Chapter headings: designs from Minton tiles by A W Pugin

Endpapers: designs after Victorian wallpapers

Colophons: designs from metalwork and tiles by A W Pugin

List of Plates

The plan shows the principal floor of that part of the Palace of Westminster which contains the Royal Apartments and the House of Lords. The rooms in which the paintings and sculpture illustrated in this book can be seen are marked by numbers (1, 2, 3 etc.), with a key.

The approach for visitors to the Palace of Westminster is by a door leading to the Norman Porch, marked ▼. The Palace is open to the public on every Saturday except the Saturday immediately preceding the State Opening of Parliament. It is also open on the following days: Easter Monday and Tuesday; Spring Bank Holiday Monday and Tuesday; Summer Bank Holiday and Tuesday; Mondays, Tuesdays and Thursdays in August; and Thursdays in September. Admission is from 10.00 to 16.30 hours.

It is also possible to attend sittings of the House of Lords as a visitor to the Strangers' Gallery. The House of Lords sits at 14.30 on Tuesdays, Wednesdays and some Mondays, at 15.00 on Thursdays, and occasionally at 11.00 on Fridays. Parliament does not sit during Recesses, which are at Christmas, Easter and Spring Bank Holiday and in the summer (usually, August and September). Visitors should join the appropriate queue outside St. Stephen's Entrance (▽ on the plan).

A Victoria Tower

B Royal Stair

C The Consort's Robing Room

D Peers' Lobby

E Central Lobby

F St. Stephen's Hall (formerly St. Stephen's Chapel)

G Westminster Hall

H St. Stephen's Entrance

1 *The Norman Porch* Busts of Lords Prime Ministers (plates 83-94).

2 *The Royal Robing Room* William Dyce's Arthurian frescoes *The Knightly Virtues* (plates 1-5); H H Armstead's wooden bas-reliefs, *The History of King Arthur* (plates 6-17) and *The History of Sir Galahad* (plates 18-23).

3 *The Royal Gallery* Daniel Maclise's Victories paintings on waterglass: *The Death of Nelson at Trafalgar* (plates 24 and 25), and *Wellington and Blücher at Waterloo* (plate 26).

4 *The Prince's Chamber* William Theed's bronze bas-reliefs of scenes from Tudor history (plates 27-38); *Tudor portraits* (plates 39-68); John Gibson's statue, *Queen Victoria with Justice and Clemency* (Frontispiece, figures i and xxvii).

5 *The House of Lords Chamber* Six frescoes (plates 69-74).

6 *The Peers' Corridor* C W Cope's *scenes from Stuart history*, fresco and waterglass (plates 75-82).

ii *Plan of the line of route in the House of Lords.*

0 ————————————— 30 m

0 ————————————— 100 ft

Abbreviations and Acknowledgements

Boase T S R Boase, *English Art 1800–1870* (1959)
Cope Charles Henry Cope, *Reminiscences of Charles West Cope,* RA (1891)
DNB Dictionary of National Biography (1921, etc)
Dyce *Centenary Exhibition of the Work of William Dyce,* RA (Thomas Agnew & Sons Ltd, 1964)
GVP *Great Victorian Pictures,* Arts Council Exhibition catalogue (1978)
KW *The History of the King's Works,* gen. ed. H M Colvin (1963 *et seq.*)
O'Driscoll W Justin O' Driscoll, *A Memoir of Daniel Maclise,* RA (1871)
Port *The Houses of Parliament,* ed. M H Port (1976)
Smith J T Smith, *Antiquities of Westminster* (1807)
Strong Roy Strong, *And when did you last see your father?* (1978)
Walker R J B Walker, *Catalogue of Paintings, Drawings, Sculpture and Engravings in the Palace of Westminster,* 7 vols., duplicated (1959–67), with 10 vols. supplements (1965–76); a set of these volumes is available in the House of Lords Record Office

I am most grateful for their help in the preparation of this book, not only to the authors of the two main sections, but also to those consulted on particular aspects of the subject, including Mr Edward Croft-Murray, Mr W Baker and Mr J C Sainty. The Gentleman Usher of the Black Rod, Sir David House, most kindly facilitated the extensive photography within the House of Lords that was needed. Much of this work was achieved with the help of Mr John Darwin, Resident Engineer and District Works Officer at the Palace of Westminster; and Mrs Hall of the Department of the Environment Photographic Library provided valuable assistance in the preparation of further illustrative material. The production of the book owes much to HMSO, and in particular to graphic design by Mr Dennis Greeno and additional art work by Mr Peter Branfield. To the assistance of the staff of both the Information and Record Offices in the House of Lords, not least to the secretarial work of Mrs Eileen Field and Miss Susan Johns, I am, as ever, indebted. Among the illustrations, figure xii is reproduced by gracious permission of HM The Queen. Other reproductions are due to the courtesy and help of the following: the office of the Lord Great Chamberlain; the Ashmolean Museum; the National Portrait Gallery; the Walker Art Gallery, Liverpool; and the Roy Miles Gallery, 6 Duke Street, St James's, London. Photography needed to complete the plates and figures was undertaken by Mr Geremy Butler, Mr Clive Friend and Mr Ken Ruder: their help, too, is gratefully acknowledged.

Maurice Bond January, 1980

Editorial Preface

The daily work of Parliament is conducted against a background of works of art. Stained glass; sculpture in wood, metal and stone; mosaic; fresco and oil painting; these media provide a complex of historical narrative and allusion designed to stimulate appreciation of Parliament's national role. When visitors come to the House of Lords to listen to debates in the Chamber they wait for admission sitting on benches dominated by a group of eight paintings of Stuart history including the Pilgrim Fathers (for the Puritan cause) and Charles I raising the standard at Nottingham (for the Cavaliers). Entering the Lords Chamber, visitors take their seats in a gallery from which they can see to left and right bronze statues of the barons who in the thirteenth century forced King John to assent to Magna Carta, and, across the Chamber, three vast frescoes recalling other events in mediaeval history, centering on the baptism of King Ethelbert by Saint Augustine. On days when the public are admitted to the main line of route in the Palace of Westminster, guides frequently find interest aroused as much by the painting of 'The Death of Nelson' in the Royal Gallery or the portraits of Henry VIII and his wives depicted in the Prince's Chamber as by the Parliamentary procedure for which these are the drop-scene.

Although the works of art at Westminster are almost entirely recent – that is, dating from the period after the fire which destroyed most of the building in 1834 – the tradition of artistic decoration at Westminster is ancient and continuous. The Houses of Parliament inherited from the Kings a Royal Palace in which to meet. No monarch has resided in what is still 'the Royal Palace of Westminster' since 1512, but in the Middle Ages it was their principal residence. It was also to a considerable extent the artistic centre of the whole country. Clearly any Palace which included Westminster Hall, second largest in Europe with arguably the finest timber roof, and above all the superb chapel of St. Stephen, the English kings' answer to King Louis IX's Sainte Chapelle in Paris, would also contain many examples of decorative art. The chapel itself was encompassed by fresco paintings with richly gilded gesso backgrounds appropriate to a splendid royal place of worship, the work from 1350 mainly of Master Hugh of St Albans.[1] Outside the chapel, in the main Palace, wall-painting had for long been the chief decorative feature – indeed the principal apartment, originally Henry III's withdrawing room or 'solar', was known for six centuries as the Painted Chamber, and the 'Court painting' there was of outstanding quality. The first of its decorations had been ordered in 1236, and the principal feature was described

as 'the great story' (a narrative painting of some type) which was supported by figures of Lions and Evangelists and by a 'Mappa Mundi', a map of the world.[2]

When Members of the two Houses of Parliament in effect became the principal occupants of the Palace in the sixteenth century they inherited this royal artistic endowment. It seemed, however, that they valued it little. The Reformation made wall-paintings of saints, angels and other religious subjects unacceptable – certainly to Puritan members of the Commons – and the first representation, engraved in 1624, of the House sitting in what had been St. Stephen's Chapel indicates that the entire wall space had by then been panelled

over.[3] Later, Sir Christopher Wren substituted far more elegant panelling.[4] A certain amount of fresco, however, was allowed to survive, perhaps because it was largely secular in character. The Court of Claims sitting in the Painted Chamber before George IV's Coronation in 1820 was depicted by J Stephanoff, and his drawing reveals a heroic size figure of a Virtue in the splay of the deep window embrasure.[5] It seems likely that similar paintings survived until the fire of 1834 in other parts of the Palace of Westminster.

Parliamentarians had probably not merely objected to religious wall-paintings as such. By the sixteenth century something richer and warmer than wall-painting was sought: the hanging of walls with tapestries. And so a second artistic tradition developed at Westminster. In Elizabeth I's reign Sir Thomas Smith noted that the House of Lords was 'richly tapessed and hanged'[6]; additional tapestries were borrowed to ornament official apartments – thus, Mr Speaker in 1628 received five tapestries of the story of Actaeon and Diana; the Lord Keeper, Speaker of the Lords, received in 1640 for his rooms in Durham House seven tapestries depicting the 'story of Hercules' and seven more showing Ahasuerus and Esther.[7] The Painted Chamber had in it a tapestry showing the siege of Troy, apparently of 15th century date,[8] and, most famous of all, the Chamber of the House of Lords was entirely surrounded by a sequence of vast tapestries, hanging from ceiling to floor. These depicted the progressive stages in the defeat of the Spanish Armada in 1588, and had reputedly been presented to the House soon after that event in the reign of Elizabeth I by the Lord High Admiral of the English fleet, the Earl of Nottingham.[9] For more than two centuries the

Lords debated within an encircling undulation of waves and a constant reminder of a foreign foe and of English victory.

So, when the fire of 1834 gave to the Houses of Parliament and their advisers the opportunity to plan and decorate a national legislature purpose-designed for the first time, they inherited an ancient tradition of wall decoration, and more particularly, of works of art of an 'historical' or 'narrative' character. The present volume seeks to illustrate the various ways and the very varying degrees of success in which that tradition has been developed since 1834 within the House of Lords and within the apartments still especially reserved for the use of the Sovereign. The Plates that follow are arranged (except for the busts) in the sequence encountered by the visitor to the Palace on public days when he or she enters at the Victoria Tower, ascends the main staircase to the Robing Room and Royal Gallery, and then is conducted through the Prince's Chamber, the House itself, and the Peers' Corridor towards the Central Lobby. Along this line of route each wall-painting and non-architectural sculpture in metal, wood or stone is described and illustrated below. The historical background to these works of the 19th century is narrated in an Introduction by Mr John Charlton, MVO, the Honorary Curator of Works of Art in the House of Lords, and formerly a Principal Inspector of Ancient Monuments. The detailed descriptions of the works of art and the rooms in which they are set are contributed by Mr Jeremy Maule, Senior Clerk in the Information Office of the House of Lords.

Away from the line of route there are very many other works of art – oil paintings, drawings, sculpture – on the walls of Committee Rooms, in ministerial and official apartments,

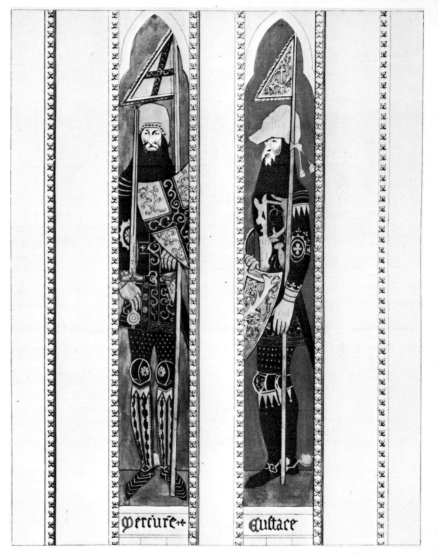

iv *Engraving of a painting of two knights on the north wall of St Stephen's Chapel.*

and also in corridors, which for the greater part are not normally accessible to the public. This extensive collection, together with a similar range of materials in the House of Commons, was for some fifteen years the subject of detailed study by Mr Richard Walker, then Curator of Pictures at the Ministry of Works (now the Department of the Environment), and at present a Cataloguer in the National Portrait Gallery. Mr Walker's *Catalogue*[10] is not only the vital scholarly background to the text of the present volume: it is also a definitive guide to the total collections in the Palace of Westminster as they stood in 1976. Its seven volumes and ten supplements, listing several thousand works of art, are unfortunately only available in a limited number of typescript copies, but the complete set can be consulted in the Search Room of the House of Lords Record Office. The Property Services Agency of the Department of the Environment hopes in due course to publish the full text of the *Catalogue,* together with supplements to date.

Meanwhile, apart from incidental references in works on art history, there is no publication to describe and illustrate in sequence the works of art within the two Houses. Interest, however, has recently been quickened in various ways and notably by a series of general studies and exhibitions. In particular, Mr Michael Port's authoritative volume, *The Houses of Parliament* (Yale University Press, 1976) included a chapter by the late T S R Boase on 'Painting', based on earlier research by him into the history of the Westminster paintings.[11] Boase, while deploring defects in technique and the quality of many of the frescoes, drew attention to what were for him two outstanding masterpieces. In Maclise's vast frescoes for the Royal Gallery 'English art in the high, romantic vein has seldom reached such narrative power and found such force and range to set it out' and elsewhere Boase praises John Gibson's statue of Queen Victoria with the figures of Justice and Mercy as 'one of the greatest pieces of English neo-classical sculpture'.[12] The whole of Boase's research with its adverse comments on Cope as well as the praise of Maclise and Gibson, has reminded specialists of the significance of the 'Westminster school' of artists. A revival of scholarly interest had been clearly signalled by the Centenary Exhibition of the work of William Dyce in Aberdeen in 1964,[13] and more recently it has received impetus from Dr Roy Strong's *And when did you last see your father?* of 1977, and additionally from the Arts Council Exhibition of 'Great Victorian Pictures' in Leeds, Leicester, Bristol and the Royal Academy in

v *The Spanish Armada: one of the tapestries which hung in the old House of Lords Chamber (detail).*

vi *Daniel Maclise at work on* The Death of Nelson, *1865, by John Ballantyne.*

vii *Albert, the Prince Consort, by F X Winterhalter.*

1978. The Introduction by Rosemary Treble to its scholarly *Catalogue* featured the 1843 exhibition of the Palace of Westminster cartoons, and the Catalogue concluded with a section on 'The Palace of Westminster Decorations'. This commented on the original 'novelty and grandeur' of the scheme, noted the technical failures which constantly recurred, but reiterated tellingly Boase's praise of the Maclise frescoes 'whose ubiquity and dramatic intensity ensured them an enduring place in the nation's visual memory'.[14]

Public interest has been paralleled by domestic care. Within the House of Lords the Offices Committee appointed in 1971 a Sub-Committee on Works of Art, which, under the Chairmanship of Viscount Hood, has been closely concerned with conservation and also with pursuing research into the 19th century sources for tiles, wallpapers, furniture and many other craft media employed at Westminster. Gradually, under the guidance of the Sub-Committee, subsequent travesties of the original Pugin conceptions have been eliminated and a return made to the designs and colours of Pugin-Hardman-Minton craftsmanship. One of the Sub-Committee's particular cares has been for the superb range of furniture designed by Pugin. A report to the Sub-Committee by the Victoria and Albert Museum on the House of Lords' furniture was published in 1974[15] – a report revealing some 325 distinct types and over 1150 pieces, probably the largest single suite of functionally designed furniture in the world. Lord Hood and his colleagues on the Sub-Committee then encouraged further publication, and with the help of HMSO, the present work is the outcome. It is hoped that besides proving of interest to those who enjoy the paintings and sculpture on visits to the House of Lords,[16] this volume will also offer material for the increasing number of historians and art specialists to whom the 'Victorian vision of the British past' is acquiring significance as a vital aspect of national history.

viii *Wall-painting of a king, from the east end of St. Stephen's Chapel.*

Maurice Bond
Information Services
House of Lords
January, 1980

Footnotes

1 *KW*,i(1963),518. William of Walsingham assisted Hugh and apparently replaced him in 1363. Margaret Rickert comments that the style was close to the Lombardic being developed in the frescoes of Altichiero and Avanzi at Padua (*Painting in Britain: The Middle Ages* (1954),169). Portions of the fresco work surviving substantially in 1807, including a remarkable Nativity, are reproduced in Smith, some in colour, and examples are reproduced here in figures 3, 4 and 8. Extensive reconstructions by Professor E W Tristram on panel of frescoes from both the Chapel and the Painted Chamber hang on the walls of the staircase and lobby leading to the Terrace of the House of Commons.

2 *KW*,i(1963),495,497.

3 The engraving was made for the Parliament which met in February 1624; it was re-used for the 1628–9 Parliament and a copy was inserted by D'Ewes in the manuscript of his *Journals* compiled in 1629–30 (British Museum, Harleian MS.73, fo.8); see J E Neale, *The Elizabethan House of Commons* (1949),404.

4 *KW*,v(1976),404.

5 The original is in Westminster City Library, Box 57, No.50A; it is reproduced in *Journal of the Society of Architectural Historians of Great Britain,* ix(1966),158.

6 Quoted in E R Foster, 'Staging a Parliament in Early Stuart England', *The English Commonwealth* (1979),135.

7 Ibid, 135–6.

8 'The very curious tapestry hung against the walls, represents the siege of Troy. Tho' the subject is Roman and Grecian, yet the buildings, dresses, warlike instruments etc. are English of the time (to appearance of Edward IV). The artists of old let ther subject be ever so remote or of what nation soever, still the buildings, dresses etc. of the time were introduc'd into their work, therefore the buildings dresses etc. seen in this tapestry are at least historical'. This quotation is from John Carter's caption to his Engraving of the Painted Chamber looking East, 1788 (Westminster City Library, Box 57, No.33A; reproduced, as noted in footnote 5 above, 156).

9 The complete series of ten tapestries was reproduced by John Pine in his *Tapestry Hangings of the House of Lords . . .* (1739).

10 See the full title of this work on p.10.

11 Notably in 'The Decoration of the New Palace at Westminster', *Journal of the Warburg and Courtauld Institutes,* xvii(1954),319–358.

12 Port,279; Boase,229.

13 Dyce, 11, speaks of the 'neglect' of his work, and the need for 'a re-appraisal of his achievement'.

14 *GVP*,92–93.

15 House of Lords Paper (1973–4),133.

16 The present publication deals with the House of Lords. The Services Committee of the House of Commons has recently announced the preparation of a book which will describe the furniture and also works of art in their own part of the Palace of Westminster, thus complementing both the Lords Report on Furniture and the present volume (Ninth Report from the Services Committee, H C (1977–78),619, para.153). Lists of the wall-paintings in the Commons are provided in the guide book, *The Houses of Parliament,* ed. B H Fell, K R Mackenzie and R B Sands (1977),pp.43–54, as well as in Walker's *Catalogue.*

Introduction
by John Charlton

The Fire and Afterwards

The accidental burning of much of the Palace of Westminster on 16th October 1834 was seen by many contemporaries as a heaven-sent chance to provide a new building in which Parliament could work efficiently and comfortably. Hitherto, trapped in a labyrinth of old buildings erected over the centuries round a royal palace, which Henry VIII had discarded as old-fashioned after 1512, generations of Parliamentarians had been considering schemes of partial improvement for over a century.

ix *The Old Palace of Westminster burning on 16th October 1834.*

Moreover the successive unions with the parliaments of Scotland (1707) and Ireland (1800) crammed the Commons chamber to bursting point, despite drastic structural alterations first by Wren and then by Wyatt. The Peers were only a little better off, despite their small numbers. Till 1800 they managed with the chamber Henry III had built for his Queen and which Guy Fawkes had tried to blow up, but with the arrival of Irish peers the House had to move to the southern part of the Court of Requests, the 'Whitehall' built in the twelfth century by Henry II. In contrast with these makeshift arrangements the Royal Courts of Justice, which for centuries were huddled in various parts of the vastness of Westminster Hall, had in 1825 been given an elegant set of courts designed by Sir John Soane and built immediately west of the Hall. The latter and the law courts were the most important structures to survive the fire (though the courts were themselves to be demolished later in the century).

The Westminster fire of 1834 also came at a time when a new spirit had entered Parliament. The passing of the Reform Act two years before had brought to the Commons a leavening of new men who saw Parliament and politics, indeed public policy as a whole, in fresh, sometimes radical ways.

The world outside Westminster was changing: the 19th century, soon to become the 'Victorian Era', was preparing for great advances in almost every field of human endeavour at home and abroad. Questions of policy, of legislation, public or private, questions about enclosures, canals, railways were becoming too important and often too complex to be dealt with simply on the floor of the House: more committees, many more committees, were needed to consider them – and committees need and

deserve appropriate committee-rooms. And there was also a call for libraries and refreshment-rooms, which had begun to be provided in the 1820s.

The fire destroyed both chambers, the Lords partly, the Commons irreparably, and made much of the rest of the Palace unusable. But government had to go on and Robert Smirke, official architect to the Board of Works, by the beginning of the new session had repaired the House of Lords to accommodate the more numerous Commons and had established the less numerous Lords next door in the Painted Chamber. This arrangement was eventually to give priority to a new Peers' chamber, since the Commons were now in fact better housed than they had been before the fire.

The expedition and skill with which Smirke had improvised tolerable if not convenient

accommodation in 1834 led at first to suggestions that he should design two new chambers between the ruins and the river-bank. These proposals were greeted with a public outcry, blazoned abroad by all parts of the Press, in which accusations of jobbery and criticisms of official architecture coincided with demands for a free competition from which could emerge a design fitting to the Mother of Parliaments. So in 1835 Smirke was dropped and on the recommendation of a select committee chaired by Lord Granville Somerset a commission was appointed to administer a competition, to be open to all comers, for a design in either the Gothic or the Elizabethan style: Gothic as being the national style, instinctively associated with the history of the race; Elizabethan, a more recent architectural fashion, which could be associated not only with Elizabeth I and Shakespeare but with that rich and over-magnificent Tudor architecture to which many 19th-century architects were attracted.[1]

Charles Barry's prize-winning entry was described by the Commissioners as bearing throughout 'such evident marks of genius and superiority of talent as fully to entitle it to the preference'[2] – a judgement that stands today. His plan was the best on all counts – a product of experience as well as genius: he well understood the requirements of buildings of public assembly, whether clubs (the Travellers, in the Classical style) or schools (St Edward's, Birmingham, in the Gothic). And the presentation of his elevations gained immensely as being by the hand of Pugin, who had already worked for him at Birmingham.

The competition result was greeted with almost as much criticism as acclaim. Much of this came from unsuccessful competitors and their supporters. But there were also doubts as to the financial management of so vast a project: the almost uncontrolled extravagance of George IV at Buckingham Palace and Windsor Castle was still fresh in Parliament's recollection. Certain alterations, too, were needed and made, in the general layout. But eventually by 1836 Barry had been appointed to build a new Palace of Westminster at an estimated cost of £865,000[3] – an immense task which he rashly promised to accomplish in about six years.

Had Barry made substantial progress by 1842 he might have been left in peace to finish the work, largely unhindered by further Parliamentary committees or commissions. But by then he was just setting the foundations. There were various causes for this delay. First was the fact that the need to keep the parliamentary machine running limited the space available for storing the great mass of materials needed. Next came the time spent on major engineering works, including a coffer-dam against high tides on the Thames, which, though vital to the necessary enlargement of the whole site towards the river, made no visual impact on the members of both Houses, who felt priority should be given to the completion of their respective chambers. Other delays arose from the appointment of an incompetent and pro-crastinating heating and ventilating engineer, the addition of certain official residences, and the occurrence of a number of strikes.

The delay gave members of the government and of both Houses the chance to meditate and to discuss the whole project. This inevitably engendered committees and commissions, including, for instance, that established 'for the Completion of the New Palace of Westminster'.[4] But vital so far as the subject of the present book is concerned, was a Fine Arts Commission appointed in 1841[5] to consider the whole question of the decoration of the interior.

The spirit which animated the members of this Commission gained strength from two causes: one social, one artistic; both moral in intention. The social element was represented by an awakened public conscience in the upper and particularly the middle classes which sought to improve by education the condition, both moral and intellectual, of the working classes. One result of this was the 'National Society for Promoting the Education of the Poor in the Principles of the Established Church', which, founded in 1811, had over 400,000 pupils twenty years later. The campaign for working-class improvement transcended party barriers, though radicals like Joseph Hume were to the fore. Art and culture were to be available to all: as more could read, there should be public libraries where workers could borrow the books they could not afford to buy; and museums and art galleries should be open on Sundays, their only day of leisure. The walls of the new Palace of Westminster seemed to present themselves as a heaven-appointed setting for examples of national art, that would tell the story of the nation at the very seat of government. And the Palace as a whole could display in its other decorations and its fittings the quality of

British craftsmanship. In addition therefore to a consideration of the general decoration of the interior there was a remarkable concentration on the artistic problem of what historic scenes should be chosen for public edification and how and where those scenes should be painted and who should paint them.

History Painting

This was in accord with a new and growing contemporary tendency. Regard for past national history and tradition had been intermittently displayed since the Restoration – in architecture, for example, by Wren and Vanbrugh. Likewise in 1739 William Kent had designed 'Gothick' screens for the Law Courts which were then huddled at the south end of Westminster Hall.[6] And it was Kent who painted for Caroline of Ansbach the group of scenes from English history now hanging in the Gothick suite he built for her husband George II at Hampton Court. For their grandson, George III, Benjamin West, the American successor of Reynolds as President of the Royal Academy, painted the vast historical canvases that now line the walls of Committee Room No. 2 in the House of Lords. But history-painting as a *genre* did not command general appeal till after the turn of the century, indeed until after the end of the Napoleonic Wars.

The prime cause of public interest in national history may be found in the immensely success-

xii *The Black Prince and the King of France after Poitiers. Benjamin West's oil now hangs in a Lords Committee Room.*

ful historical novels of Sir Walter Scott, which treated historical characters as real people, the incidents of whose lives could be all the more exciting because they were concerned with actual historical events, their lives gradually unfolding in the imagination of the reader. Soon the reader's mental images were given form with the production of illustrated editions. With this interest in historical incidents went also an interest in the details of life in historic times. Evelyn's diary published in 1818, may have been one factor; but the publication of Pepys' Diary seven years later, incomplete and bowdlerised as it was, greatly stimulated popular demand, which among other things produced over the years more and more complete editions, each a best seller. Perhaps the best seller of all was the first volume of the *History of England* by Thomas Babington Macaulay, later one of the members of the Houses of Parliament Fine Arts Commission. Nor was the concern with national history limited to middle and upper class adults: children's books on national history, with illustrations, could be found in their households. In 1826 John Murray had published an illustrated edition of Mrs Markham's *History of England . . . with conversations at the end of each chapter*; and Lady Calcott (aunt of J C Horsley, the painter of *Religion* in the Lords' Chamber[7]) in her *Little Arthur's History of England* (1838) appealed to mothers and governesses to make the teaching of national history part of early training.

The pictures in these books, whether for old or young, might be simplified copies of famous historical paintings (like the 16th century painting of Henry VIII leaving Dover for the Field of the Cloth of Gold) or they might be specially drawn. If the latter, they increasingly depended on the researches of antiquarians into such matters as early costume and furniture represented in mediaeval effigies or wall-paintings or derived from funeral monuments. Gone were the carefree 'Gothick' days of Kent and West. With the growing demand for antiquarian correctness in representation, the 'history painter' of the day had to have in his mind or ready to his hand an apparatus of antiquarian scholarship which could be sometimes a hindrance rather than an inspiration; and in an artist such as William Dyce could lead to a kind of antiquarian paralysis.

The appointment of the Fine Arts Commission

The Fine Arts Commission of 1841 and the Parliamentary Committee which led to its appointment represented the culmination of a movement for the involvement of government in

xiii *The conversion of King Ethelbert, from* Little Arthur's History of England *(1838): the Anglo-Saxons were a popular subject in the 1843 competition.*

the Arts which had begun in the early 1830s. It first had active expression in the Ewart Committee of 1835[8] which reported on the connection between arts and manufactures and led to the setting up of government schools of design at Somerset House in 1837. In its report the Ewart Committee had hoped that Government patronage might extend to fresco painting, as the noblest of the visual arts, a hope eventually realised in 1841 when the President of the Board of Trade, Henry Labouchere (later Lord Taunton), himself an art collector, asked Parliament for a grant for experiments in that medium. A month later a Select Committee to consider 'the promotion of the fine arts in this Country in connexion with the rebuilding of the Houses of Parliament' was set up by the House of Commons with William Ewart and Henry Labouchere among the members and Sir Robert Peel in the chair. The rest of the members were mainly distinguished amateurs with a general knowledge of the arts.[9]

At its first meeting the Committee found its opening witness, Charles Barry, somewhat unresponsive. He may have felt that the Committee's knowledge of art history was too much for him; but he must also have had doubts about the suggested imposition on his building-programme of a painting scheme intended for walls as yet unbuilt, let alone ready for such artistic exercises. Next to appear was Sir Martin Shee, President of the Royal Academy, who among other things favoured the use of fresco. His views were endorsed by the Aberdonian painter William Dyce, Director of the new Government School of Design, who, as will be seen, had some knowledge of this technique and of its revival by the German 'Nazarenes' in Rome and later in Germany. Another witness, Charles Eastlake (one day to be both President of the Royal Academy and Director of the National Gallery) was also acquainted with the German practitioners and the organisation of their work. He thought that English artists, duly instructed, could paint in fresco. Later in the year Cornelius, the leading German exponent of the revived fresco technique, visited England and had discussions with Eastlake at Peel's suggestion. Finally, in November 1841, a Fine Arts Commission was appointed to take in hand the whole question of the interior decoration of the New Palace. This was to be an external and not a Parliamentary body. Although it included

24

Parliamentarians like Viscount Melbourne, the former Prime Minister and political instructor to Queen Victoria, and Viscount Palmerston, recently Foreign Secretary, the Commission also numbered among its members several who had sat on the Commons Select Committee, among them Peel, and from the world of scholars and from the arts men such as Henry Hallam the historian and Samuel Rogers the poet. Eastlake was to be Secretary and the Chairman Albert, the Prince Consort.[10]

The Prince Consort

The choice of Prince Albert in 1841 as Chairman was surprising but inspired, and his influence on the revival of arts and crafts at Westminster was a prelude on a small scale to his efforts in the national field which resulted in the Great Exhibition of 1851 and the ultimate establishment of the museums of Kensington.

In 1841 Prince Albert had only been resident in England for a year. In 1840 he had married Queen Victoria, his cousin. They shared a Saxe-Coburg uncle, Leopold, first King of the Belgians, the widower of Charlotte, Princess Royal, whose death in 1819 in effect opened the way to the Princess Victoria's accession. Much of King Leopold's life was devoted to promoting the interests of the Saxe-Coburg family, mainly by a series of royal marriages, and that between Victoria and Albert was to be his greatest triumph.

As they grew up Leopold had kept in close touch with the upbringing of the two young people. Victoria was somewhat insulated from his instruction by her position as an English princess near the throne and by the English Channel, but circumstances placed the education of Albert almost wholly in the hands of King Leopold and of his personal adviser and

xv *The third page of the Commissioners' Fourth Report (1845): signatures of Prince Albert and others.*

fellow Coburger, Baron Stockmar. From adolescence onwards this involved Albert in foreign travel, accompanied by tutors and pursued by admonitory letters, so that by the time he was twenty he had visited most of the great cities in Europe. These were no pleasure-trips, but opportunities for study and as such took in the great art collections, to the study of which not only his mentors but his own inclinations led him. It was in these circumstances that in Italy and Germany he saw not only the paintings of old masters, but the history-paintings of a recent school of artists known as the Nazarenes.[11]

xvi *The Prince Consort underemployed in the early 1840s. Queen Victoria was at first anxious to keep Prince Albert out of politics, but 'Protocols' and 'Fresco' are among the lures tempting the Prince to future activity.*

PUNCH'S PENCILLINGS.—N°. XXI.

CUPID OUT OF PLACE.

From a Sketch made in "The Palmerston Gallery."

It was on his return to Brussels from one of these foreign pilgrimages that he tried his 'prentice hand at history painting, choosing as his subjects three characteristic scenes of combat. The most ambitious echoes the Nazarene interest in Goethe and national history: a scene from the poet's early history-drama about Gottfried von Berlichengen. The two small pictures portray the Death of Count Mansfield and Romeo Provoking Tybalt.[12] Amateurish as these paintings may appear, they yet show a sense of crisis, of a particular dramatic moment in history or drama, which was a special feature of history-painting and one which at Westminster the Prince must later have recognised particularly in the work of Cope. Moreover their execution should have given the Prince an insight into the practical as well as the artistic

problems of putting paint on canvas. With these experiences behind him it seems natural that when the Fine Arts Commission met the Prince should have 'entered with enthusiasm upon the labours'.[13]

His practical knowledge apparently extended to the existing state of the academic art-world, for when he was invited by Peel to head the Commission one of his conditions was that Charles Eastlake should be its secretary.[14] Eastlake was not only a practising painter but a man of broad artistic interests with whom the Prince had much in common. Indeed several paintings by Eastlake were to grace the royal sitting-room at Osborne. A born administrator, supported by a formidable wife, he became President of the Royal Academy in 1850 and Director of the National Gallery five years later.[15] It was in this last post that the Prince convinced him of the importance of the Italian and German primitives, with which he was enriching the royal collection but which were hardly represented at the National Gallery. Despite the burden of duties inseparable from his additional responsibilities Eastlake remained an active secretary of the Commission. For example it was his intervention with the Prince that brought the latter to Westminster to persuade Maclise from resigning his commission to paint the great frescoes in the Royal Gallery. But his devotion to duty had its price and, like the Prince and Barry, he died of overwork; so that by the middle sixties three of the main actors had stepped from the Westminster scene.

The Prince Consort's appointment as Chairman of the Fine Arts Commission set him on a course he was to follow with increasing devotion for the rest of a busy life: the promotion of the arts and crafts and their practical application. He became president of and re-vivified the Royal Society for the Encouragement of the Arts and Manufacturers (now the Royal Society of Arts) and the Government School of Design, of which William Dyce was Director, could rely on his enthusiastic support. These activities were eventually to blossom into the Great Exhibition of 1851. At Westminster, however, the craft side of the Palace was firmly in the grasp of Charles Barry, leaving the Prince the arts of painting and sculpture.

The Prince had always got on well with artists, having a natural sympathy with their ideals and problems. Lady Eastlake (wife of the secretary to the Commission) said in an obituary notice in 1861 that 'no artist employed in the works of the Commission ever approached the Prince without recognizing a clearness of perception, regarding the principles and purpose of art, which contrasted curiously and refreshingly with the vague and often false conventionalities to which the votary of art is generally doomed as a listener'.[16] His approach to his Westminster team was both sympathetic and businesslike: he gave them personal commissions.

The major commissions went to Dyce – a fresco and two religious pictures for Osborne. Cope produced for the Prince his vast canvas of 'Cardinal Wolsey dying at the gate of Leicester Abbey', which the Prince hung at Osborne overlooking his billiard-table (for which he had designed a 'functional' base with decorations in the style of Raphael). And it was to Osborne that he took Horsley's 'L'Allegro', which he bought when the Commission had rejected it as an entry for Miltonic subjects to be painted in the Upper Waiting Hall at Westminster, because Macaulay insisted that only incidents from 'Paradise Lost' were eligible. Another instance of his concern with the Westminster artists has already been mentioned: his relations with Maclise (who also had a commission from the Prince). When the artist was in despair over the technical difficulties confronting him in painting his Royal Gallery frescoes the Prince came up specially from Osborne, persuaded him to withdraw his resignation and go to Berlin where

xvii *A meeting of the Fine Arts Commission in 1846.*

he was converted to the waterglass technique in which the paintings were finally executed.[17]

Unfortunately the Prince's interest in painters and sculptors, scientists and engineers, did not seem to extend to architects – least of all to Sir Charles Barry. He must have been perfectly well acquainted with Barry's work at Trentham Park for the Queen's great friend and Mistress of the Robes, the Duchess of Sutherland, and have climbed Barry's magnificent staircase in Stafford (now Lancaster) House.[18] But when what was known as the Queen's Marine Residence at Osborne was built – and in an Italianate style – he turned instead to the London builder, Thomas Cubitt, a plain practical man whose personality and prompt and economical business methods appealed to him. For more sophisticated advice on its decoration he relied on his artistic adviser, Dr Grüner, who had associations with the Nazarenes.

This distrust of Barry was also felt by most if not all of the other members of the Commission in the 1840s who experienced Barry's determination to insist on his authority as architect to the building and must have considered this as obstructive to their main purpose – the display in the new palace of British art, whether pure or applied.

Thus their secretary, Eastlake, wrote to the Treasury in 1846:

'The Architect has undertaken on his own responsibility the whole of the decorative work in reference to several of the objects comprehended in the [notices to Artists issued by the Commission in 1843] with the exception of Stained Glass, though even in this branch the Artist recommended by the Commission has been instructed by the Architect to adapt his designs instead of following his own conceptions'.[19]

Later the Prince is quoted as saying 'every step Sir Charles [Barry] takes requires careful watching'.[20]

The deaths of the Prince and Barry removed these two antagonists from the arena and signalled the effective end to the Commission, though its deliberations and reports continued for a few years after 1861. But their major decisions as to subjects, painters and locations had been taken. A number of the paintings the Prince did not live to see. As it is, they are in a sense a better memorial to his taste and his determination than the monument in Kensington Gardens.

Fresco Painting

Some regarded and many still do regard, however, the major decision of the Prince and his fellow Commissioners to use *fresco* at Westminster as disastrous. This is a process in which pure powdered pigments, mixed in water, are applied to a wet freshly laid lime-plaster face. It was an ancient medium, dating back at least to Minoan Crete and referred to by Pliny and Vitruvius. It had been used by Michelangelo and Raphael for their greatest works and it had always carried with it a prestige beyond that of oil painting. This depended partly on the broad simplicity of treatment (appropriate to large-scale works) and to the purity of the materials used. During the eighteenth century however the chemistry of painting began to change – colours, for example, needed no longer to be hand-ground, they could be had ready-made; there was more awareness of the effect of pollution on paintings in large cities and painters themselves seemed to be retiring into their studios. At the same time the teaching of art was becoming hidebound.

In reaction against this early in the nineteenth century a new painting cult had been established in Rome. Housed in a ruined monastery, calling themselves the Brotherhood of St Luke and nicknamed, as we have noticed, the Nazarenes, its members were Germans who wished to replace the existing methods of art-teaching by something approaching the apprenticeship of mediaeval times.[21] The rule of the academy had a strong religious flavour and in its teaching moral and aesthetic principles seem to have held an equal place. As the century advanced both masters and disciples gradually spread over Germany, though one of their leaders, Overbeck, was still in Rome and must have met the Prince Consort when he visited that city. But the most famous member at that time was Peter van Cornelius, who decorated for King Ludwig I of Bavaria the palaces of Munich with frescoes in the Nazarene manner and was regarded as the 'schoolmaster of Europe' in matters of fresco. It was Cornelius whom the 1841 Commission and its representatives consulted, not indeed so much on aesthetics as on methods of production, which at Munich were highly organised.

To one of its witnesses Cornelius had put the case for fresco on general grounds as follows:

'It is difficult to impress upon the mind of a nation at large a general love of art unless you were to use as an instrument Painting upon a large scale, and Fresco was particularly suited for this purpose: it was not to be expected that the lower classes of the community should have any just appreciation of the delicacies and prior characteristics of painting in oil, and that they required large and simple forms, very direct action, and, in some instances, exaggerated expression.'[22]

The Commission's attachment to fresco depended, however, not just on its propriety as a medium for historical exposition but on various practical grounds. For example, the shiny surface oil painting reflected, while the matt surface of fresco did not; and the problem of reflection was a serious one in view of the scale of the proposed paintings. And the Commissioners were impressed by the theory, which proved lamentably untrue in practice, that frescoes could easily be cleaned by the use of stale bread. But the biggest practical issue was a human one: apart from William Dyce none of the painters to be involved in the work at Westminster had any experience of working in fresco.

Here it may be appropriate to insert a description of the process as seen by a writer of the time.

'In executing paintings in fresco the necessary preparations are the sketch, the cartoon in full size cut in suitable pieces, – the colours prepared with water only, and the two sorts of plaster, the rendering and finishing coats on which the picture is to be painted. The painter's mind must be full of his subject; everything must be pre-determined on, as no alteration or amendment can take place: he must have a rapid and decisive execution, and be well acquainted with the qualities of his colours, as they dry lighter when laid on. There are two operators, the plasterer in constant attendance, and the painter who follows him, and dyes or embues his colours into the very body of the plaster whilst it yet be wet . . . . The colours must be dashed on at once, in a broad, bold and general manner, that with an able artist must produce a grand style'.[23]

The Nazarenes, though they regarded Rome as in a sense their spiritual home, a religious and artistic focus which Germany lacked (many indeed were Roman Catholics or converts), and though they thought religious painting the highest art, were conscious of their national history, and Dürer and Goethe were their national artistic and literary heroes. When, therefore, leaders of the school such as Cornelius and Schnorr were asked to advise on the Westminster frescoes, which were also to deal with national history, their eventual recommendation was that British artists should be chosen, despite suggestions that Germans should be employed.[24] Of British painters, as has been seen, only Dyce had had much experience of the style and technique of the Nazarenes. He had stayed with them in Rome in 1827–8 and was held in high esteem by them; so that Cornelius is said to have told the Prince Consort: 'What need have you of Cornelius to come over and paint your walls when you have got Mr Dyce?'.[25]

The Fine Arts Competitions

In 1843 the Commission announced a competition (with various money prizes) for cartoon drawings 'executed in chalk or charcoal, not less than ten or more than fifteen feet in their longest dimension; the figures to be not less than the size of life, illustrating subjects from British history, or from the works of Spenser, Shakespeare or Milton'.[26] The 140 entries were displayed in an exhibition, attended on 3 July 1843 by Queen Victoria, in Westminster Hall. This proved immensely popular with the public, for whom 6d and 1d explanatory pamphlets were provided. Of the successful competitors, however, only C W Cope and J C Horsley were eventually employed in the Lords. Of the subjects chosen, more than half were mediaeval, with a strong leaning towards two highly disparate subjects, pre-Norman Britain and John Milton, the latter outnumbering Shakespeare and Spenser combined by some 40 entries.

In 1845, with the Chamber of the House of Lords nearing completion, the Commissioners announced a limited competition for frescoes to be painted in the arched spaces at either end of the Chamber. Poetic subjects were dismissed (to appear later – and eventually decay – in the Upper Waiting Hall of the House of Commons) in favour of History. The final scheme comprised three allegorical paintings of Justice, Religion and Chivalry, in that order, on the north wall (that viewed by the Sovereign during the opening of Parliament) while on the south wall (viewed by the assembled company on that occasion and above the throne) were to be historical exemplifications of those virtues: Prince Henry acknowledging the authority of Judge Gascoigne; the baptism of King Ethelbert; and King Edward III conferring on the Black Prince the Order of the Garter.

Six artists – Dyce, Maclise, Cope, Horsley, Richard Redgrave and W C Thomas – were invited to make cartoons and do samples of fresco, though with no guarantee of subsequent employment. In spite of this move the Commission held a further and open competition in June 1845, followed by one for oils as late as 1847.[27] These well-intentioned but indecisive endeavours to discover all possibil-

xviii *The cartoons submitted for the competition of 1843 on display in Westminster Hall.*

ities brought about more than parliamentary criticisms of delay – they discouraged the abler competitors, who had more profitable outlets for their talents than submitting proposals (in a new painting technique) for pictures they might never be asked to paint. As a countermeasure, the Prince Consort had given commissions to a number of painters which represented the field from which the final Westminster choice might be made. These were to paint in a summerhouse in the grounds of Buckingham Palace a series of scenes selected from Milton's *Comus* and Sir Walter Scott's *Waverley Novels*.[28] Finally as a matter of urgency Dyce, Maclise, Cope and Horsley were selected to prepare frescoes for the House of Lords. Some of the other competitors were to get commissions in the Commons part of the Palace. Painting could now begin.

Wall Paintings after 1845

The first commission for a fresco went appropriately enough in 1845 to Dyce, one of the main advocates and practitioners of that medium. To him was assigned the only Anglo-Saxon figure-subject, that of the Baptism of Ethelbert, to be painted in the arched panel above the throne. Dyce first took a 'refresher-course' in fresco by visiting Italy, where he met Cope and Horsley similarly employed.[29] But when they started, the painters encountered many difficulties, for masons and plasterers were still at work in the Palace of Westminster. By the end of 1847, however, four paintings had been finished, the last two, Cope's *Judge Gascoyne* and Maclise's *Justice* being completed in 1849. As the first Westminster paintings to be executed they suffered not only from adverse conditions of work, but from being in a sense unprecedented attempts to work on a large scale. Their

subsequent history has almost inevitably been one of repeated restoration. Much of the colour has gone and their artistic interest lies rather in the cartoon, the actual design, and the ideas which lay behind it. Otherwise, the pictures' unobtrusive tones match the mellowness of their splendid surroundings in the House of Lords Chamber.

With their Report on monumental sculpture completed in 1845, and the Lords Chamber itself opened (to enormous public approval), the Commissioners were free to set about planning historical painting in the rest of the Palace. At

xix *Punch's Own Picture: a satirical view of work under way on Cope's fresco of Prince Henry.*

the time of their Seventh Report (July 1847), the impact of the new Palace on the public was at its height. The *Illustrated London News* had described the Lords Chamber interior as 'the finest specimen of Gothic civil architecture in Europe', and pronounced of the Prince's Chamber '.. we doubt whether even King Louis [i.e. Ludwig] of Bavaria, that art-loving Monarch, ever imagined a more perfect specimen of art-decoration'.[30] The Commissioners now produced grandiose schemes for covering with historical fresco every square inch of wall available.

But all too soon they had to cut their coat according to their cloth. Parliament for some time had looked askance at the delays and expenditure which their activities involved; Barry himself had little sympathy with the inevitable interference with his overloaded programme. And the Commission itself was running out of steam. Peel, its prime mover, died in 1850, the Prince Consort became increasingly involved in the Great Exhibition of 1851 and though the devoted Eastlake remained secretary, his election as President of the Royal Academy encroached upon his time – an encroachment enhanced when five years later he also became Director of the National Gallery.

However, the major projects in the House of Lords were duly allotted, all to original (and therefore experienced) members of the existing team. In August 1848 Dyce was given the Story of King Arthur for the Royal Robing Room; in 1853 Cope was given a series on Stuart history for the Peers' Corridor; and in 1859 Maclise was given the commission, in fact to provide wall decoration for the whole of the Royal Gallery, which eventually resulted in his two great panoramas of Waterloo and Trafalgar.

A subsidiary but prominent scheme was the series of Tudor portraits in the Prince's Chamber carried out in the 1850s under the superintendence of Richard Burchett of the Department of Science and Art, South Kensington. Beneath them was to be a series of bronze relief panels depicting famous events of the period by William Theed the Younger, a favourite sculptor of the Queen and Prince Albert. These and the Arthurian wooden panels carved by H H Armstead in the Royal Robing Room in the 1860s are discussed later.

For the Royal Robing Room Barry, as the architect of the New Palace, had at first thought of tapestries as the main wall-surfaces, but he later turned to historic events in the lives of earlier sovereigns. The Commission's leanings had for some time been towards Chivalry – a motif already in the Lords' Chamber. The Prince might have preferred the Anglo-Saxons, from whom he considered he sprang and for whose virtues he had a high regard. Eventually, Arthur and his knights were chosen as the subject and in 1848 Dyce contracted to paint seven frescoes – all to illustrate the life and times of that legendary period – instances of what were thought to be the seven knightly virtues.

Arthur was recognised by the educated public as a heroic figure in national history, worthy to stand, admittedly in a somewhat shadowy way, with other national heroes like King Alfred. The main literary source was of course Malory's *Morte D'Arthur* (which Dyce followed), but Tennyson's *Morte d'Arthur* appeared in 1842, Thomas Wright's edition of Malory in 1856, and Tennyson's *Idylls of the King* (dedicated to the Prince Consort) in 1859. A parallel revival of Arthurian interest may be seen in paintings by Rossetti and others in the Oxford Union building from 1857 onwards.

Sixteen years later Dyce had completed only four large frescoes in the Queen's Robing Room when he died in 1864. His prolonged occupation of an apartment intended for the use of the Queen at the opening of Parliament was noted by the Commissioners in their annual Reports, where they apologised for the 'great inconvenience to Your Majesty'. It was also reflected in the fact that for later years of his life the artist's address was given in the Royal Academy year-book as the Royal Robing Room, House of Lords!

Dyce gave two reasons for his slow progress. The first, probably the more irritating to the artist, was that, unlike his patriotic sea-piece at Osborne, his subjects at Westminster demanded historical verisimilitude in the matter of the costume of the figures he was to paint. No one knew what Arthurian costume (presumably of the sixth century) was like and the ladies could be dressed in simply flowing robes, but knights needed to appear in armour.

Antiquarian studies of armour suggested that chain mail, if not used in the sixth century, was at any rate the earliest form of such protection, so in chain mail the Arthurian knights were clad; but the artist complained bitterly of the time it took to paint. In the later years Dyce could claim that ill health played its part in his delay, but one factor he did not mention. This was the series of religious frescoes he was painting for William Butterfield's brilliant and revolutionary Church building at All Saints, Margaret Street – a congenial task for which he readily left King Arthur and his court.

The second difficulty concerned the whole use of fresco – and this was a problem for all the Westminster artists and needs further consideration. Dyce had been abroad to reinforce his knowledge of the laying on of fresco and

xx–xxi *'A great quantity of chain mail' delayed Dyce's work on the Robing Room frescoes of the Arthurian legend.*

produced a technical report, published by the Commissioners, which dealt with such problems as the effects of damp and candle-smoke. Other artists, Horsley and Cope, also went abroad, the latter spending much time at Munich discussing with the Nazarenes the frescoes they had executed in that city. Maclise did not; he took least kindly to fresco, though his Lords Chamber paintings are skilful exercises in the Nazarene manner. He was highly critical of the difficult conditions in which it had to be used at Westminster. (A rough pencil sketch by Cope showing Maclise at work on one of his paintings there is labelled 'Maclise Fresco Painting under difficulties. House of Lords'.)[31] A crisis came when he refused to transfer the painting of Wellington and Blucher (to be described below), to the walls of the Royal

xxii *Music-making at Arthur's court – a detail from Dyce's* Hospitality.

Gallery. He said he 'felt disgusted at the dry and rigid materials for his production' and longed for oil. He also complained about the patches of colour thrown on the wall he was painting by the stained glass in the windows. The Prince Consort came up from Osborne to interview Maclise and persuaded him to visit Berlin. Here a new medium for wall-painting had been adopted instead of the daily instalments required by fresco. The whole painting was fixed by spraying with waterglass. Maclise was convinced by what he saw in Berlin and the panoramas in the Royal Gallery were painted by the Waterglass or Stereochrome method. Cope too, then at work in the Peers' Corridor, used this method for his later pictures. Only Dyce soldiered faithfully on by the old method in the Royal Robing Room.

With hind-sight the conclusion seems to be that whether painted in fresco or waterglass the Commission's grand scheme was ill-fated from the start, for conditions at Westminster could hardly have been more unfavourable to the painters. The very air was against them: a damp English climate accentuated by fogs and sewer gas from the Thames meant fresco-painting could dry only in a few months of the year. Charles Barry, as architect but not a member of the Commission, was concerned only with the completion of his design and the maintenance of the everyday business of Parliament. He had his own work to do and this did not include attendance on the painters, who were plagued by the dust and noise of building-work. Nor, indeed were the walls to which the plaster for their painting was applied necessarily dry enough for the purpose. Before they were finished some of the paintings required restoration or repair. These sad extracts from the reminiscences of Horsley and Cope show how splendid hopes were brought low and the painters were sick at heart:

'How vain was all our work, our keen enthusiasm, our greatest efforts, which in some cases absorbed the very flower of our youth . . . none of us knew that fresco-painting required not only fresh plaster on which to work, but fresh air to preserve the work when done. The Thames was the main sewer of vast London and . . . was charged with foul and most destructive gases. Moreover, the present terrace of the Houses was then the site of a vast workshop, where hundreds of workmen, working day and night, necessitated the consumption of unknown volumes of coal gas, which was pouring forth its destructive powers night and day . . .'[32]

'. . . On looking back through the years I feel how much of life has been wasted in, as it were, writing in the sand. Time's effacing fingers began to obliterate at one end, while we were painfully working at the other'.[33]

Sculptural Work

As has been said earlier, the terms of reference of the Fine Art Commissioners were not confined to painting: they were meant to embrace all such decorative arts as would embellish the interior of the New Palace and display the excellence of British design and craftsmanship. The National School of Design at Somerset House, for example, should have the opportunity to make its contribution. So craftsmen and designers in stained glass and metalwork, wood-carving and encaustic tiles, indeed architectural sculpture, were invited to submit proposals. Here, however, the Commissioners reckoned without the architect, for Barry considered he had all he needed in the way of designers, executants and contractors. He had Pugin, whose genius of invention far outran the talents of all competitors; he had John Thomas to organise the vast programme of architectural sculpture; and he could lay his hands without the Commissioners' prompting on the right contractors: Hardman for glass and metalwork, Minton for tiles, Crace for general decoration – all firms of the highest competence which had already worked for him and with Pugin.

The first contest came over the Lords' Chamber, the completion of which was badly needed for both practical and ceremonial reasons. There were differences over the design of the stained glass for the tall windows, which were meant to contain a series of royal figures. After a series of contradictory decisions the Commissioners awarded the contract for the design to the Edinburgh firm of Ballantine & Allan. The cartoons they produced were as ill-executed as their subjects were ill-conceived – the latter, for example, included the figure of Henry II holding a bleeding heart 'to denote that he died of a broken heart, caused by the

xxiii *The Lion and the Unicorn: one of many versions at Westminster designed by Pugin.*

undutiful behaviour of his children'.[34] Barry would have none of this, had the figures re-drawn by Pugin and replied to the Commissioners' complaints by pointing out that Ballantine & Allan's contract contained a clause, providing for the rejection of their work should it not come up to standard, which it manifestly did not. The firm was, however, allowed to manufacture the glass, apparently to Barry's satisfaction. The outcome of this contest over stained glass seems to have established Barry's authority over the general decoration of the interior, apart from paintings and detached sculpture, the effect being to produce a unity which, thanks to Pugin's inexhaustible fund of invention, could be felt in every aspect of the New Palace.

The question of sculpture in the House of Lords itself was, however, a matter of friction. The design provided for the series of statues of Magna Carta barons which today lines the

upper level of the Chamber. To the Commission this series appeared as detached sculpture; they selected (after some disagreement among themselves) suitable barons and a group of distinguished sculptors was commissioned. But to Barry these figures were part of the architecture of this major interior and they must accord with the general proportions of the whole. He got his way by designing the niches, in which the figures stand, in strict relationship to the rest of the interior – narrower that is than the sculptors wanted – one of whom explained when the barons' narrow shoulders were criticised that 'Mr Barry will not allow us room for them'.[35]

Barry and the Commission were, however, at one over the proposal, happily abortive, for a series of free-standing white marble royal statues extending from the Royal Entrance to the Prince's Chamber. Seven only were executed – in the '60s after the deaths of the Prince Consort and Barry. They were James I,

Charles I and II, William and Mary, George IV and William IV. They proved too massive for their setting and their places in the Royal Gallery were shortly taken by the present statues of victorious sovereigns carved by J B Philip and set in niches designed by Edward Middleton, second son of Charles Barry and his successor as architect to the New Palace. The rejected monarchs were then moved to Westminster Hall, where they may be seen lined up against the east wall in a photograph of Mr Gladstone's lying-in-State.[36] In 1913 a Select Committee presented them to the Corporation of the City of London and then in 1915, after a brief sojourn in Guildhall, they found their present resting-place in the entrance hall of the Central Criminal Court, Old Bailey.[37]

Some of the most effective work in sculpture now surviving at the House of Lords, however, is not free-standing work but carving and moulding in deep relief. Most notable of all are the bas-reliefs carved in oak by H H Armstead which tell the story of King Arthur. These were commissioned in 1866 to complement the Dyce frescoes already in place in the Royal Robing Room above, much as Theed's reliefs illustrating Tudor history had earlier done with the royal portraits in the Prince's Chamber. Armstead had already executed six statues of Kings (Alfred, William I, Henry II, John, Henry VIII and William III) elsewhere in the Palace – in New Palace Yard – in the late '50s, but he was probably best known for his work on the Albert Memorial and his statue of G E Street in the Law Courts. His training, however, had not been that of a conventional sculptor and it is perhaps to this that the vigorous plastic quality of his work in the Robing Room may be ascribed.[38]

An old student of the Government School of Design at Somerset House he joined the famous gold and silver smiths, Hunt and Roskill, where he rose to be chief designer and gained a wide reputation for his sculptural designs in the field of metalwork. Certainly his talent in this field is displayed to advantage in his Robing Room panels, particularly in contrast with Dyce's rather static frescoes above. Armstead's weirdly vivid reliefs have a graphic intensity which prompted a contemporary critic to compare them with the work of Blake. Here indeed is the Dark Age world of Arthur and his Knights. Dyce's Arthur is really that of Tennyson's *Idylls of the King:* Armstead's is that of Merlin.

Armstead's reliefs are today out-distanced in popular esteem by the bronze reliefs of Theed in the Prince's Chamber – which are not only better lit and more easily seen but deal with a less mythical past than the age of King Arthur. Their sculptor, William Theed the Younger (1804–91), was, like Gibson, *persona grata* with the Prince Consort, who had acquired some of

xxv *Engraving of John Thomas' architectural sculpture,* St George, *at the crown of the Royal Entrance Arch.*

xxvi *William Pitt, Earl of Chatham: commissioned by the women of England and America in 1915.*

his work and had given him various commissions. Queen Victoria continued this royal favour after the Prince's death in 1861. It was Theed who made the Prince's death-mask for the Queen, as well as the main memorial bust.[39]

Of sculpture as it is more generally known, busts and full length statues in stone or metal, the House of Lords has less to offer. Most on the public line of route are grouped at the beginning of the processional way through the building, in the Norman Porch.

The busts are of noble Prime Ministers. They stand on the surrounding plinths and are recent arrivals at Westminster, generally by gift. They include some meritorious sculpture: Joseph Wilton's 'Earl of Chatham', Thomas Campbell's 'Lord Grey' and the 'Duke of Wellington' by E H Baily, sculptor of the statue of Nelson's column. Politically they are a useful reminder of the times when the Prime Minister was more likely to sit in the Lords than the Commons.

The dominant work of sculpture, however, is placed in the Prince's Chamber: the group showing Queen Victoria, flanked by figures of Justice and Mercy, which is depicted in the frontispiece to this volume and is described in detail below. Its sculptor, John Gibson, RA (1790-1866) was the son of a Conway market-gardener. He began as a mason, but early showed promise in and devotion to sculpture. Despite much encouragement in this country his great ambition was to go to Italy even 'if he went on foot' and in 1817 he arrived in Rome where, apart from an occasional visit to England, he remained till he died, a venerated figure, in 1866. On his arrival he was befriended by Canova, then the master of the neo-classic style, and later by Thorwaldsen and he was probably the last important exponent of their style. A childlike soul, not to be trusted on a railway journey lest he lose himself, his luggage or both, but a master in his own studio, he had a special appeal for the Prince Consort, who seems to have regarded him as the most reliable of British sculptors. With William Theed the Younger, whose Tudor-period reliefs also appear in the Prince's chamber, he was commissioned to do the high-relief sculptures in Pennethorne's Supper Room at Buckingham Palace. And later he was to advise on the Albert Memorial.

There could never have been any question of Gibson adapting the style of his sculpture of the Queen to the Gothic profusion surrounding it, but his throne at least, set against its diapered background, pays respect to tradition in a certain Gothic flavour in its shape.[40] Queen Victoria presides centrally within what may fairly be described as the outstanding work of Victorian architecture in the land.

Decay and Conservation

The subsequent history of the works of art executed at Westminster between 1840 and 1870 has been far from happy, but before summarising its main stages two caveats should be entered. First, the sculpture, whether in metal or wood, has naturally been exempt from decay. The work of Gibson, Theed and Armstead at Westminster speaks to the public as well today as a century ago. Secondly, the medium that has attracted almost continuously bitter criticism – that of fresco – is notoriously difficult and frequently impermanent. Frescoes at Pompeii, as for instance those in the Villa dei Misteri, show that the best work technically can triumph over the passage of time, but all too many later masterpieces in fresco are today a shadow of their original splendour. Modern guide books describing the greatest of all sequences of wall-paintings, those by Cimabue, Giotto and others in the Basilica of Saint Francis at Assisi, briefly but accurately summarise some as 'considerably perished', others as 'damaged, mutilated and completely erased'. Perhaps the most famous wall-painting of all, that of the Last Supper by Leonardo in the refectory of Santa Maria delle Grazie in Milan, was found to be deteriorating after 20 years, was further damaged by 'hasty, ill-advised attempts at restoration' and is today in a 'sorry state'. These are admittedly works centuries older than the Westminster paintings; but the story of

xxvii *The Useful Arts, in which Gibson shows a steam-engine, a telegraph-wire and 'other useful objects'; bas-relief at the foot of* Queen Victoria, Justice and Mercy.

wall painting, to some extent like that of painting in oils but certainly unlike that of sculpture, can be one of rapid decay and then of inexpert restoration.

'Time's effacing finger' was only too apparent in the last century to the painters at Westminster even as they worked – perhaps most tragically in the case of Maclise, who saw the brilliant colours of his widely acclaimed *Wellington and Blücher* fading before his eyes as he painted the *Death of Nelson*. Indeed the unhappy labour of his demanding (and ill-paid) Westminster commitments not only discouraged him from accepting the presidency of the Royal Academy, but probably contributed to his death in 1870. Dyce, another embittered soul, had died six years earlier – only Cope and Horsley were then left. Men in their sixties, they subsequently strove to restore as best they could not only their own work but that of Dyce and Maclise – an act of artistic filial piety which has ensured that the paintings retain more than a little of their original conception, despite the various restorations which they have since had to undergo.

The restoration-history falls into four main periods: that done by the painters to their own pictures in their lifetime, as in Dyce's work on his *Ethelbert*. Secondly, what is best described as an act of loyalty to the Westminster school of history-painting: cleaning, retouching or re-painting and re-fixing by Cope and Horsley (with assistants) from the late '60s to about 1880 (by which time they were both old men). This work might be granted a kind of authenticity of restoration from the old painters' recollection of what was originally intended. Then, the third stage might be called the reign of Sir Arthur Church, who was Professor of Chemistry at the Royal Academy from 1879 to 1911 and well known to Cope and Horsley. Church carried out two campaigns of cleaning, some retouching in tempera and waxing in 1894/5 and ten years later. Lastly, some fifty years ago the picture conservation studio of the former Office of Works (now the Department of the Environment) assumed responsibility for the Houses of Parliament paintings. Cleaning and treatment with preservatives have since then continuously been carried out at Westminster by that studio.

The chronicle of the treatment accorded the paintings has been thoroughly recorded by Mr Richard Walker in his catalogue.[41] Here comment must be limited to major restorations during the four periods of conservation.

Dyce had led the way in fresco painting, and his work was one of the first to decay. In 1862, while trying to finish his *Hospitality* in the Queen's Robing Room he was given permission to restore his *Ethelbert,* painted in 1846 above the throne in the House of Lords. How much he did is uncertain, but ten years later (and six after Dyce's death) Cope and Horsley, with Frederick Wright the chemist as scientific adviser, were voted £300 to carry out a general repair. Since then the *Ethelbert* seems only to have been cleaned and waxed.

Matters were no better in the Queen's Robing Room, where Dyce had completed four out of seven paintings in 1851–54 but, for various reasons recounted above, left the fifth (*Hospitality*) unfinished at the time of his death in 1864. If it seems ironical that the work of the British master of fresco should be the first to decay it should be remembered that he alone remained faithful to the medium; his other Westminster colleagues had all turned to the waterglass method. In response to the petition of Dyce's widow, Cope finished *Hospitality,* at the same time repainting two of the heads in waterglass. Two years later he washed and waxed it and it passed inspection till in 1894 Prof Church reported it as badly decayed and the paint loose. It was cleaned, touched up with tempera and waxed; since then it has only been cleaned. Cope was commissioned to carry out a general repair of the other four Dyce paintings in 1866–67. *Mercy,* he reported, was the most imperfect and in a filthy condition, and two heads had to be cut out and repaired. This restoration lasted till 1895 when Church found the painting very dirty and his cleaning involved touching up with tempera. The story of the other paintings is similar, varied with occasional details of features having to be repainted, as, for instance, the head of Sir Launcelot and the sword of Sir Bors (*Generosity*).

Professor Church's restoration work in 1894 seems to have been the most drastic of all over the past century. *Religion* for example was entirely repainted in tempera; even so it required 'a good deal of repainting' in 1905. Subsequent treatment of the series has been limited to cleaning. It should be added that the Robing Room faces due south and that these, alone in the Palace paintings, have had for many years to withstand a high intensity of natural light.

The work of Maclise caused probably even more concern than that of Dyce. Maclise's *Chivalry* (completed 1847) and *Justice* (1849) in the House of Lords Chamber soon went the way of their companion pictures, deteriorating almost from the day they were finished. Here once again Cope and Horsley rallied to what they must have felt to be a lost cause, cleaning and retouching in 1874, four years after Maclise's death. Professor Church was active in

1895, but did no repainting, and later treatment seems to have been limited to cleaning. Indeed at close quarters the paintings seem to preserve more of their original 'Nazarene' flavour than the others in the Lords.

But it is Maclise's great waterglass paintings of Waterloo and Trafalgar in the Royal Gallery that tell the saddest tale, though even in their present almost monochrome state they win the acclaim of the general public and also of art-historians. Maclise's change of technique from fresco to waterglass had given the painter greater facility in executing his great panoramas but had done little to slow down their deterioration. Indeed in the last year of his life a critic could say 'We eagerly look forward to the removal of these unfortunate frescoes which year by year blacken on the wall'. A letter from the First Commissioner of Works seeking his counsel came too late for action: Maclise died that year. Four years later a Committee under Lord Hardinge bowed to criticism in *The Times* by arranging that the paintings should be cleaned by George Richmond. His method was to beat them with slings of linen and wash leather and pads of cotton wool 'delivered with all the force that a man could give a side stroke'. This failed and was succeeded for some years by the gentler method of periodic cleaning, varied in 1890 by blasts of air from a bellows. Professor Church supervised general treatment, including the use of paraffin wax and varnish, but apparently no repainting was undertaken. Finally, a comprehensive scheme of restoration was carried out by the Ministry of Works Conservation studio in 1962–64, and this has produced, it seems, a stable condition with no very evident signs fifteen years later of further deterioration.

Horsley's solitary piece of work has had a happier history. The fresco in the House of

Lords of *Religion* was finished on 14 April 1847, the day before the Chamber was used for the first time for the Opening of Parliament. In 1873, after chemical washing by Wright the previous year, the artist was paid fifty guineas for repair-work, for the necessity of which he blamed the gas-jets in the Chamber. He pointed out that his frescoes painted at Somerleyton in 1848 were 'as fresh as the day they were painted' – Dyce could have said the same about his fresco at Osborne. Church cleaned it and touched it up with tempera but did not repaint and there was some further restoration by the Ministry of Works in 1950–51.

The artist who had had the longest association with the Westminster paintings and their conservation was C W Cope. This association dated from the time when he had won a premium of £300 in the 1843 competition.

In 1856 Cope duly began his eight paintings for the Peers' Corridor in fresco, but in 1862, when halfway through, he changed to water-glass. This, of course, was what Maclise had done, but it also corresponded with a leprous outbreak of decay on the arm of the girl in the boat in his fresco *Pilgrim Fathers,* finished as recently as 1856. As in the case of Maclise the change to waterglass gave the artist greater freedom in the application of his paint but little help in the matter of preservation. Neither did the portable slate frames devised by Barry which were intended to provide a circulation of air behind the pictures. Eventually in 1874–75 Cope repainted the pictures where necessary in waterglass and they were glazed as they are today. As late as the year 1880 Cope, now in his seventieth year, was cleaning his fresco *Prince Henry* in the House of Lords with the help of his son A S Cope. This seems to have been the only treatment it received until 1950–51. In 1878 he

reported that its companion piece, *Edward III conferring the Order of the Garter on the Black Prince,* was decaying beneath a crust of London grime, but it was not till 1893, three years after his death, that his son was employed in 'entirely repainting the whole picture', retaining as far as possible the original colour scheme. This fresco too seems to have been left alone until 1950–51.

Neither the zeal of the artists, nor *ad hoc* Parliamentary enquiries really solved the problem set by wall-paintings. Continuous supervision allied to climatic control were to prove the best answers and perhaps the single most important step was the establishment in 1927 by H M Office of Works of a conservation studio under the late Mr J F S Jack. This meant that the Westminster paintings no longer had to wait for angry parliamentary or public comment before they received attention. In the subsequent half-century the wall paintings have been periodically inspected and treated when necessary. But a still greater step forward has been environmental. The passage of the Clean Air Act in 1956 (amended in 1968) vastly reduced the noxious vapours coming in from the sulphur-laden London atmosphere which were inevitably circulated by existing heating and ventilating systems in the building. Furthermore the progressive introduction of electric heating increasingly reduces the damage that can be done by air-currents, and the fact that some of the air circulating in the House of Lords – certainly that in the Chamber – is air-conditioned is making for a more favourable environment. Hesitantly, it can be hoped that the worst is now over, and that within this improved climate the conservation studio can continue to maintain the wall-paintings if not in their original state, at least in one that has a reasonable chance of stability.

Footnotes

1 *KW*,vi,574ff.

2 Parl. Papers, H C, 1836 (66),xxxvi.

3 Estimates summarised in Port,88.

4 Appointed 1848. Among the members was Lord de Grey, first president of the Royal Institute of British Architects.

5 See below, pp.23–5.

6 In 1755; *KW*,v,390.

7 She had wanted Horsley, then 18, to illustrate the book, but his great-uncle, Sir Augustus Calcott, RA, said he was too young. R B Gotch, *Maria, Lady Calcott* (1937),291.

8 The Select Committee on Arts and Manufactures, Parl. Papers, H C, 1835,v,375; 1836,xxi,43.

9 Parl. Papers, H C, 1841,vi,331.

10 T. Martin, *Life of the Prince Consort,* i,(1875),123.

11 There is a general description of the Prince's tour in Martin, *op. cit.,* chapter ii, based in part on the papers of Baron Stockmar, noted there, 18,f n 3.

12 They are now at Osborne.

13 Martin, i,123.

14 J Steegman, *Consort of Taste* (1950),137.

15 D N B.

16 *Quarterly Review,* cxi (Jan 1862).

17 O'Driscoll, 149.

18 The reference here is to the staircase-hall, decorated by Barry, not to the actual stairs.

19 Public Record Office, Works. 11/9/4 f38.

20 General Grey, secretary to the Prince Consort to (Sir) Henry Cole, closely associated with the Prince over e.g.

the 1851 Exhibition (Cole Papers, box 1, Victoria and Albert Museum).

21 Keith Andrews, *The Nazarenes* (1948).

22 H T Ryde, *Illustrations of the New Palace of Westminster* (1849),57.

23 Ryde, *op. cit.* 55 n.

24 Andrews,85.

25 Andrews,84.

26 Parl. Papers, H C, 1842, xxv (412).

27 T. Boase in *Journal of The Warburg and Courtauld Institutes,* 17(1954),331f.

28 Martin, *op. cit.,* 167ff. An illustrated account of the pavilion was published by Dr Grüner at the time.

29 Cope, 150,165.

30 *Illustrated London News,* (1847)x,282.

31 Illustrated in Port, 273.

32 J C Horsley, *Recollections of a Royal Academician* (1903),266f.

33 Cope, 257.

34 Quoted in Port, 247.

35 Port, 233.

36 National Portrait Gallery, *Sir Benjamin Stone, 1838-1914* (Exhibition Catalogue),32.

37 Walker,iii,107.

38 *D N B.*

39 *D N B,* R Gunnis, *Dictionary of English Sculptors* (1953), 386 and references there.

40 Gibson's own description of the throne is in T Matthews, *The Biography of John Gibson* RA (1911),177.

41 Documentation for statements in this concluding section is to be found in Walker,iv.

xxviii–xxix *Royal portraits now occupy the panels never filled by fresco in the Royal Gallery: King William IV and his Queen Adelaide.*

xxx–xxxi *Queen Elizabeth II and Prince Philip.*

I The Royal Robing Room

A Descriptive Narrative,
I to VI
by Jeremy Maule

When George IV ascended the throne he called at once for immediate alterations in the House of Lords. What had always been a Royal Palace should have, at the least, proper facilities for the monarch; and accordingly Sir John Soane re-planned and built a Royal Gallery, Royal Staircase and ante-chamber, apartments which he had first designed for George III in 1794–95. By March 1824 Soane could report that 'The approach for His Majesty to the House of Lords is completed': and although much of the scheme perished in the fire of 1834, the idea that the Houses of Parliament should contain chambers, gallery and staircase suitable for the estate and dignity of the monarch in Parliament was well established.

When Barry had won the competition to become the architect of the New Palace, the Robing Room was one of his first concerns. On 23rd September, 1836, he sent to Pugin tracings of the King's Robing Room, Gallery and Staircase and asked him to 'set about immediately'. Barry's plan and Pugin's designs for the interior ran into heavy criticism in the Lords, led by Lord Sudeley. The final shape of the Royal rooms of the Palace was the result of discussions between Barry, various junior ministers, Prince Albert and the Prime Minister, Peel, who finally carried the day for a plan which would enable the young new Queen to appear at the Opening of Parliament with the maximum of ceremony – 'such an arrangement of the Royal Robing Room as shall enable the Sovereign to pass through the Victoria Gallery direct to the House of Lords in the Robes of State'.

At Barry's death in 1860 the Robing Room was by no means complete. Work was still in hand on the fireplace, the stained glass, the parquet floor and in the spaces left for Dyce's wall-painting. By 1870 these were occupied either by Dyce's frescoes or by Armstead carvings which filled up the frieze panels that Dyce never began.

The result is one of the most integrated rooms in the New Palace and one not unduly large – it is 54 feet (16·48 m) long and 37 feet (11·29 m) wide. The ceiling is coffered in the style of Henry VIII and is decorated with heraldic stencils by Pugin on which the personal emblems of the Kings of England are featured (Richard II's hart, Henry VI's swan, Henry VII's Beaufort portcullis and others). The walls beneath display in succession interlaced design, a band of arms of the Queens of England, some of Pugin's richest wall-papers interspersed with gilt statuettes, and then Tudor linen-fold panelling within which Dyce's frescoes and Armstead's carved reliefs are set. The foliage in stained glass is to the design of Pugin's son-in-law, J H Powell. At the further end of the room is a small chair of state on a dais surmounted by a richly embroidered backcloth of 1856 embroidered with the Royal Arms and Queen Victoria's monogram by the Royal School of Needlework. Facing it is a fireplace by the younger Barry, very much in Pugin's style. The grate is surmounted by royal arms, backed by Minton heraldic tiles, and defended by two gilt fire-dogs – a lion and a unicorn bearing (detachable) standards. Crocketted finials, canopy and flanking figures of Saint George and Saint Michael complete the piece.

This rich and elaborate room is now used annually by the Sovereign who here assumes the Royal Parliamentary robes and the Imperial State Crown, before walking in procession through the Royal Gallery, preceded by the Great Officers of State, and entering the Chamber of the House of Lords for the State Opening of Parliament. From time to time the room has had additional uses: certain committees and conferences were held here in the 1930s, and when in 1941 the Commons Chamber was destroyed, the Lords gave up their own Chamber to the Commons and the Royal Robing Room, being fitted with benches and galleries, then served until 1951 as the House of Lords Chamber.

Monograms and carved prayers in Latin for the Queen's safety make this a Victorian room, but it is also Arthurian.

The Robing Room is the starting point for the procession of the crowned and robed Monarch in Parliament. In parallel, King Arthur, the subject of its frescoes and carvings, represents the moment which Victorians conceived as the starting point of their national history. The works of art reproduced in plates 1 to 23, the frescoes of William Dyce and the bas-reliefs of H H Armstead, are all inspired, as has been described in the Introduction, by Malory's romance of King Arthur. Indeed, the feeling that King Arthur was the first of our national heroes has a notable ancestry. When in 1344 Edward III sought to form an order of chivalry he 'began his Round Table in the same manner and conditions the lord Arthur, formerly King of England, appointed it, namely to the number of 300 knights'. A Round Table house was built in Windsor Castle, the Round Table made for it is probably that now in Winchester Castle, and it was only the outbreak of the Hundred Years War and a sudden need for more saintly patronage that caused Edward III after the triumphs of Crécy and Calais to make his new Order of Chivalry that of Saint George.

More recently there has been a strong revival of interest in Arthur. Not only has a great deal of archaeological and historical investigation been carried out, but writers from John Masefield and Charles Williams to R C Sherriff, Alfred Duggan and T H White have made Arthur once more a popular hero. The starting point to national history suggested by the Robing Room at Westminster is again acquiring general significance, for in the words of one archaeologist it was 'a period of the greatest importance for the island . . . because it decided the cultural and linguistic make-up of Britain'.

References

KW, vi, 519–525; E W Pugin, *Who was the Art Architect of the Houses of Parliament?* (1867),23–24; Port, 109, 252–53; W St John Hope, *Windsor Castle* (1913, 3 vols.); M Pointon, *William Dyce 1806–1864* (1979).

1 *Courtesy*

William Dyce, 1852, fresco, 11 ft 2½ in × 5 ft 10 in
(3·42 × 1·78 m)
Walker, iv, 33

Sir Tristram harping to La Beale Isoud

The fresco illustrates the knightly virtue of Courtesy, as exemplified in Sir Tristram's courtly skill of harping and his love for Isoud.

The episode comes early in the Book of Sir Tristram, when the knight has sailed to Ireland to be cured of a poisonous wound. Isoud (or Isolde or Yseult, as she is also known in the story), the King's daughter, has healed him and is described by Malory as 'at that time the fairest maid and lady of the world'. She is shown standing under an arch. Sir Tristram, renowned for his harping and the proto-type of courtly love, 'learned her to harp and she began to have a great fantasy unto him'.

2 *Mercy*

William Dyce, 1854, fresco, 11 ft 2½ ins × 10 ft 2½ ins
(3·42 × 3·11 m)
Walker, iv, 34

Sir Gawain swears to be merciful and 'never to be against ladies'

The fresco depicts the virtue of Mercy and illustrates a curious story, early in the *Morte d'Arthur*.

Sir Gawain, angry at a knight who had killed his hounds, refused mercy to the knight and prepared to cut off his head. 'Right so came his lady out of a chamber and fell over him, and so he smote off her head by misadventure.' Gawain is ashamed, and back at Court tells this story against himself. Queen Guenever makes him swear upon the four Evangelists 'that ever he should be courteous and never refuse mercy to him that asketh mercy . . . and that he should never be against lady nor gentlewoman'.

46

3 *Religion*
William Dyce, 1851, fresco, 11 ft 2½ in × 14 ft 6 (3·42 × 4·43 m)
Walker, iv, 31 (see also Dyce, 52 and plate x)

The Vision of Sir Galahad and his Company

The fresco which depicts the prime knightly virtue of Religion was the first of the series to be finished, in 1851. It illustrates the passage in Sir Thomas Malory's *Le Morte d'Arthur* in which the three pure knights who alone of Arthur's Court were to succeed in the Quest of the Holy Grail see a vision in a hermitage. Sir Galahad, Sir Perceval and Sir Bors de Ganis, together with Sir Perceval's sister, see a vision of Jesus Christ and the Four Evangelists. Each of the Evangelists appears with his traditional symbol (from the Book of Revelations): lion, eagle, ox and man.

4 *Generosity*

William Dyce, 1852, fresco, 11 ft 2½ ins × 5 ft 10 ins (3·42 × 1·78 m)
Walker, iv, 32

King Arthur unhorsed by Sir Bors and spared by Sir Launcelot

The scene depicted is from the closing passages of Malory's *Le Morte d'Arthur* and illustrates, in Malory's words, 'the great courtesy that was in Sir Launcelot more than in any other man'. The fresco shows an episode from the siege of Sir Launcelot in his castle of Joyous Gard by King Arthur and Sir Gawain. King Arthur is shown thrown from his horse by Launcelot's kinsman, Sir Bors, who meant to have killed him. Launcelot spares Arthur: 'Not so hardy', said Sir Launcelot, 'upon pain of thy head, that thou touch him no more, for I will never see that most noble king that made me knight neither slain nor shamed'.

5 *Hospitality*
William Dyce, unfinished at his death in 1864,
completed by C W Cope, 1864–6, fresco,
11 ft 2½ ins × 21 ft 9 ins (3·42 × 6·64 m)
Walker, iv, 35–6

The admission of Sir Tristram to the Fellowship of the Round Table

The fresco of knightly Hospitality illustrates one of the finest passages of Malory's prose. Sir Tristram, after many adventures, is brought to Arthur's court by Sir Launcelot, and welcomed there:

'Then King Arthur took Sir Tristram by the hand and went to the Table Round. Then came Queen Guenever and many ladies with her, and all the ladies said at one voice: Welcome, Sir Tristram! Welcome, said the damsels. Welcome, said knights. Welcome said King Arthur, for one of the best knights, and the gentlest of the world, and the man of most worship. For all manner of hunting thou bearest the prize, and of all measures of blowing thou art the beginning, and of all the terms of hunting and hawking ye are the beginner, of all instruments of music ye are the best; therefore, gentle knight, said Arthur, ye are welcome to this court'.

6 *The Birth of King Arthur in the Castle of Tintagelle*
H H Armstead, bas-relief in oak, 1870, $23\frac{3}{4} \times 26$ ins
(60·42 × 66·14 cm)
Walker, iii, 103

Queen Igraine is shown lying on her bed, having given birth
to a baby boy. King Utherpendragon, the father of the child,
holds up his new born son.

7 *Arthur Delivered unto Merlin*
H H Armstead, 1870, bas-relief in oak, $23\frac{3}{4} \times 28$ ins
(60·42 × 71·23 cm)
Walker, iii, 103

On the advice of Merlin the infant Arthur was made over to
the care of one of King Utherpendragon's knights, Sir
Ector. The panel shows Merlin disguised as a poor man
receiving the child at the postern gate of the castle and
preparing to take him away for christening.

8 *Arthur recognised as King*

H H Armstead, 1870, bas-relief in oak, $23\frac{3}{4} \times 28$ ins
($60 \cdot 42 \times 71 \cdot 23$ cm)

Walker, iii, 103

The young Arthur draws the sword from the stone in the churchyard of St Paul's, while the Archbishop of Canterbury looks on. The commons cry aloud 'We will have Arthur unto our King – for we all see that it is God's Will'.

9 *Arthur crowned King*

H H Armstead, 1870, bas-relief in oak, $23\frac{3}{4} \times 27\frac{1}{2}$ ins
($60 \cdot 42 \times 69 \cdot 96$ cm)

Walker, iii, 103

Arthur, fresh from knighting, is crowned King of England by the Archbishop. Orb in hand, he swears to the Lords and Commons 'to be a true King' and 'to stand with true justice from thenceforth all the days of his life'. The Lords of the Kingdom do him service.

10 *The Battaile with King Lot*
H H Armstead, 1870, bas-relief in oak, $23\frac{3}{4} \times 27\frac{1}{2}$ ins
(60·42 × 69·96 cm)
Walker, iii, 103

King Lot of Orkney and the other Kings of the outlying
small kingdoms of Britain resisted Arthur's leadership: in
the Battle of Eleven Kings, King Lot and King Arthur fight
hand to hand.

11 *How King Arthur gate [got] his Sword Excalibur*
H H Armstead, 1870, bas-relief in oak, $23\frac{3}{4} \times 26$ ins
(60·42 × 66·14 cm)
Walker, iii, 103

An arm, clothed in white samite, holds the sword of power
Excalibur above the waves of a lake. Arthur, supported by
Merlin, leans down from the barge to take the gift of the Lady
of the Lake.

12 *King Arthur wedded to Guenever*
H H Armstead, 1870, bas-relief in oak, 23¾ × 56 ins (60·42 × 142·46 cm)
Walker, iii, 103

At a high feast in Camelot Arthur is wedded to Guenever, both standing under a cloth of estate. Escorting ladies, knights and pages complete the scene.

13 *King Arthur conquering the marvellous gyant*
H H Armstead, 1870, bas-relief in oak, 23¾ × 57 ins (60·42 × 145 cm)
INSCRIBED H Armstead
Walker, iii, 103

Armstead's most imaginative scene shows Arthur locked in struggle with the giant of Brittany, who had ravaged that duchy for seven years. His latest victim, the Duchess, lies dead; and by her side three maidens kneel and 'call to Christ for help and comfort'. With the aid of his two knights Arthur overcomes the giant.

14 *The Knights of the Round Table vowing to seek the Sancgreal* H H Armstead, 1870, bas-relief in oak, $23\frac{3}{4} \times 56\frac{1}{2}$ ins (60·42 × 143·74 cm) Walker, iii, 103

The carving shows the Knights of the Round Table after a miraculous vision of the Holy Grail on the feast of Pentecost. In various postures, kneeling, swearing on their sword, or with hand raised, they vow to pursue the Grail in Quest. Arthur stands at their head, saddened by the break up of 'the fairest fellowship and truest of knighthood'.

15 *The Misadventure of the Adder – Beginning of the Battaile* H H Armstead, 1870, bas-relief in oak, $23\frac{3}{4} \times 56$ ins (60·42 × 142 cm) Walker, iii, 103

As the opposing forces of Arthur and his treacherous son Sir Mordred meet before the battle, a knight, stung by an adder, draws his sword to strike the snake. At the sight of the drawn sword, both sides blow trumpets and Arthur signs the last battle to begin.

16 *Sir Mordred Slaine – King Arthur wounded to death*
H H Armstead, 1870, bas-relief in oak, 23¾ × 56 ins (60·42 × 142·46 cm)
Walker, iii, 103

The carving shows the field at the battle's end. Malory says, 'And never was there seen a more dole-fuller battle in any Christian land'. Mordred, slain by his father's spear, lies among a heap of dead bodies of men and horses. Arthur, fatally wounded by his son's sword, is supported from the field by the two other survivors, Sir Lucan and Sir Bedivere.

17 *King Arthur carried in a barge to Avillon attended by Queens*
H H Armstead, 1870, bas-relief in oak, 23¾ × 56 ins (60·42 × 142·46 cm)
Walker, iii, 103

King Arthur, is carried to the waterside by Sir Bedivere; 'and there received him three queens with great mourning'. Accompanied by other ladies in black, the King leaves in their barge for the Vale of Avillon to heal his wounds. Bedivere stands disconsolate at the edge of the lake.

18 *Sir Launcelot leaving Dame Elaine*
H H Armstead, 1870, bas-relief in oak, 23¾ × 28 ins
(60·42 × 71·23 cm)
Walker, iii, 104

Sir Launcelot as a guest of King Pelles, whom Malory describes as cousin to Joseph of Arimathea and guardian of the Grail, has been tricked into spending the night with the King's daughter Elaine. When he reproaches her, she tells him that his son will be the noblest knight of the world, Galahad. 'And so Sir Launcelot arrayed him and was armed, and took his leave mildly at that young Lady Elaine.'

19 *Sir Galahad brought unto the Siege Perilous*
H H Armstead, 1870, bas-relief in oak, 23¾ × 28 ins
(60·42 × 71·23 cm)
Walker, iii, 104

Sir Galahad is brought unarmed by a good old man to King Arthur's Round Table. He is being led to the Perilous Seat, where only the best knight in the world may sit. On the seat are found the words: 'This is The Siege of Galahad, the haut prince'.

20 *Galahad receives the Sword with the Strange Girdels*
H H Armstead, 1870, bas-relief in oak, $23\frac{3}{4} \times 24$ ins
$(60\cdot42 \times 61\cdot06$ cm)
Walker, iii, 104

Galahad, flanked by two knights, receives a miraculous sword.

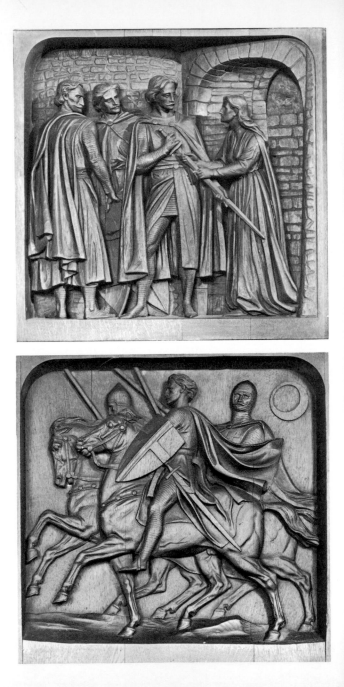

21 *Sir Galahad, Sir Percivale, Sir Bors*
H H Armstead, 1870, bas-relief in oak, $23\frac{3}{4} \times 24$ ins
$(60\cdot42 \times 61\cdot06$ cm)
SIGNED H H Armstead Sculpt
Walker, iii, 104

A year and a half after the quest of the Sangreal had begun, the
three knights who are to achieve it come together, and ride to
Castle Carbonek where they meet with King Pelles and the Grail.

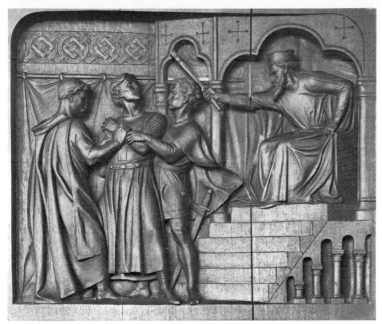

22 *Sir Galahad imprisoned by the tyrant*
H H Armstead, 1870, bas-relief in oak, 23¾ × 28 ins
(60·42 × 71·23 cm)
Walker, iii, 104

Sir Galahad, Sir Percivale and Sir Bors arrive at the spiritual city of Sarras and tell the King 'the truth of the Sangreal, and the power which that God had set there'. The King, a pagan tyrant, has them thrown into prison.

23 *Sir Galahad's Soul borne to Heaven*
H H Armstead, 1870, bas-relief in oak, 23¾ × 29 ins
(60·42 × 75·05 cm)
Walker, iii, 104

Sir Galahad, crowned as King of Sarras, had died at the end of Mass, celebrated by Joseph of Arimathea in the likeness of a bishop. 'And then', says Malory, 'suddenly his soul departed to Jesus Christ, and a great multitude of angels bare his soul up to heaven.' A hand from heaven takes up the Grail; the Quest is achieved; and 'since then was there never man so hardy to say that he had seen the Holy Grail'.

II The Royal Gallery

The Royal Gallery presents the most martial aspect of the chambers of the New Palace of Westminster. It was also for long the least used. From the start, the idea of a processional gallery had met with criticism from many peers, who wished the Queen to be able to pass straight from her Robing Room to the Parliament Chamber. And even when its existence had been agreed upon, its purpose gave rise to further debate. Soane's original plans in George III's reign had envisaged 'the rooms leading into the proposed new House of Lords as a *depot* for Sculpture, commemorating great public actions . . .' As it turned out, this was not far from the eventual decision of the Royal Commission, announced in their Seventh Report of 1847, which recommended as suitable for the decoration of the Royal Gallery subjects relating 'to the military history and glory of the country'.

The Commission's first plans seem to have been for every wall of this immense chamber 110 feet by 45 feet by 45 feet (33·58 × 13·74 × 13·74 m) to be covered in fresco. In 1844 Peel had told Lord Sudeley 'My own opinion is decidedly in favour of the Victoria Gallery being appropriated to the encouragement of the Art of painting . . .' When the Commission came to report, they took Barry's suggestion that the wall-space should be divided into eighteen compartments, and suggested appropriate subjects for each. These ranged from Boadicea and Alfred to Nelson and Wellington, and represented a much more balanced selection than the original cartoons submitted for the Competition of 1843. However, Albert and the other eight members of the Commission's Committee did choose some of the earlier award-winning subjects, including Selous' *Boadicea* and Severn's *Eleanor sucking poison from the wound of Edward*.

It was not till 1857 that detailed arrangements were made to begin the work. The Prince Consort wished Maclise to be employed, and in correspondence with Eastlake the artist suggested the Royal Gallery, 'as containing subjects, on the whole, more interesting to me'. He began with designs for the two large compartments, each 45 ft 8 ins (13·94 m) in length, and the cartoon of Wellington meeting Blücher after the battle of Waterloo was exhibited at the Royal Academy in 1859. It was almost the only painting in the whole Palace that met with universal approbation. Forty-three of his fellow-artists presented him with a gold porte-crayon as a token 'of the honest pride which, as artists and fellow countrymen, we feel in the success of the cartoon you have lately executed'. But within a month Maclise had resigned his commission. The perplexities of practical execution were listed in a letter to Eastlake: chief among them were the difficulty of joining the elaborate uniforms as each day's small portion of fresco was added to the next and the problems posed by the Gallery's stained glass. 'When the sun did *not* shine', he wrote, 'I could barely see, and when (it did) the heraldic devices ..... griffins, dragons and all – in gules, and gold, and azure, were emblazoned in form and colour over the forty-six feet of compartment, shaming and falsifying, in their dazzling passage over them, my poor earthy lime-burnt tinges.'

Prince Albert acted with typically swift resolution. He wrote at once to Eastlake, urging persistence – 'a grand historical work requires the sacrifice of these details; and fresco is a protection to Mr Maclise against himself, and insures his rising by this work to a height as an artist which he cannot himself comprehend as yet'. He promised the stained glass should come out, and drew an elaborate diagram of reflectors, designed to diffuse light over the compartments concerned. Finally he came up from Osborne to interview Maclise in person and sent him to visit Berlin and report on the latest waterglass techniques in use there. The Prince Consort carried the day. Maclise was completely converted to the new technique, which enabled him to work on a prepared ground to which the finished painting was eventually fixed by spraying with alkaline silicate. The Waterloo scene was finished in 1861 and unveiled in March 1862. At once another problem arose. Had the legendary meeting ever taken place? Eastlake consulted the Queen; the Queen consulted her daughter, now Crown Princess of Prussia; the Princess consulted the aged General Nostitz, Blücher's aide-de-camp, and the General consulted his memory. All was well.

Only one other painting was completed by Maclise although he worked with what the Commission described as 'unremitting industry'. This was the Death of Nelson. The oil sketch (shown here in colour as the original waterglass is now much faded) was completed in February 1863 and the whole work finished in 1865. The remainder of Maclise's contract was cancelled and the reticent artist never received payment for the three designs prepared for small compartments in the Gallery. The glass of which Maclise complained was never removed – Prince Albert's death intervening to save the griffins – until it was blown out in the Second World War.

The remainder of the wall space in the Royal Gallery is today occupied by portraits of Monarchs and their consorts from King George I to Queen Elizabeth II. They are mainly copies of originals by Kneller, Reynolds, Lawrence and other artists. The most recent, those of the Queen and Prince Philip, are by Sir James Gunn and A C Davidson-Houston, respectively. An attempt in 1924 to introduce panel paintings that would complement Maclise's led to designs being prepared by Sir Frank Brangwyn which were however criticised by the Royal Fine Art Commission as not harmonizing with their surroundings. The panels now are in the Assembly Hall of Swansea Corporation.

Although at first little used, the Royal Gallery has gradually become an extremely useful Parliamentary apartment. The State processions through it for the Opening of Parliament began again in 1901, and since 1959 have frequently been televised thus making the Gallery one of the better known features of the Palace. As the largest convenient assembly place apart from Westminster Hall, it has also been used for many receptions, when Commonwealth Prime Ministers and foreign

Heads of State have addressed both Houses assembled here. And on public days it provides visitors with space in which to circulate and also to inspect the architectural model of the ancient Palace displayed there. In addition, since 1979, the Royal Gallery has housed a permanent exhibition of Parliamentary documents arranged by the Lords Record Office. It has thus become very fittingly the home of the most important constitutional document in the land after Magna Carta – the Declaration of Rights of 1689 on which modern constitutional monarchy is based.

References

KW, vi, 520–1; Port, 106, 109, 281; Journal of the Warburg and Courtauld Institutes, xvii (1954), 329 ff.; O'Driscoll, 145; Walker, iii, 1 and 128, supp. v, 3 and supp. vi, 5; *The Records of Parliament 1497 to 1977* (House of Lords, July 1979). A copy of Lord Sudeley's *Observations on the plans for the New Houses of Parliament...* (1844), presented by the present Lord Sudeley, is now held in the House of Lords Record Office.

25 (overleaf) *The Death of Nelson*
Daniel Maclise, waterglass painting:
12 ft 1 in × 46 ft 8 ins (3·69 × 14.25 m)
Walker, iv, 69–70; see also O'Driscoll, chapter xii and *Daniel Maclise* (Arts Council of Great Britain, 1972), 113–114.

The *Death of Nelson* shows the dying Admiral, supported by Captain Hardy, on the deck of the Flagship *Victory* at the Battle of Trafalgar, England's conclusive victory in 1805 over the naval forces of Napoleon and his Spanish allies. Among the group surrounding Nelson are Dr Beattie, Captain Adair, Lieutenant Ram, Sergeant Secker of the Marines and a sailor bearing the ensign of a captured ship. In his efforts to obtain authentic details, Maclise had studied portraits, made innumerable drawings and interviewed survivors from the Battle of Trafalgar, among them Captain Parker and Admiral Seymour who had both been midshipmen on the *Victory*. The rest of the massive picture is full of details of the carnage of sea-battle – among them the sniper aloft on the French ship; a woman bathing a bleeding sailor's head; and the dazed desperate look of a young powder-monkey.

26 (overleaf) *The Meeting of Wellington and Blücher after Waterloo*
Daniel Maclise, waterglass painting,
12 ft 1 in × 45 ft 8 ins (3·69 × 13·94 m)
Walker, iv, 66–8; see also O'Driscoll, chapters x, xi and *Daniel Maclise*, 109–113.

The central scene shows Wellington, mounted on his charger Copenhagen, meeting with the Prussian Marshal Blücher at the farm La Belle Alliance after the battle of Waterloo, Wellington's signal and final victory over the French Emperor, Napoleon. By Wellington, mounted, are shown Lord Arthur Hill (afterwards Lord Sandys), General Somerset and the Hon Henry Percy, who carried home the dispatches and captured Eagles. Near them are soldiers of the Life Guards and 1st Regiment of Horse Guards Blue, one holding aloft the Blues' tattered standard (now in Chelsea Hospital). Next to Blücher are Gneisenau, who carried out the pursuit, Bülow, Ziethen, Nostitz and a black Brunswicker in dark green uniform and death's head cap. Maclise had been to immense pains to authenticate details of uniforms (specially made by the War Office), weapons (studied at the Tower of London) and the faces of the prominent figures (copied from portraits and sketches lent by Prince Albert and others). His only minor inaccuracy appears to be the inclusion of an ophicleide in the military band – an instrument not invented till 1817.

24 (opposite) *The Death of Nelson*
Detail from oil sketch for 25, by Daniel Maclise.
Reproduced by courtesy of the Walker Art Gallery, Liverpool.

25

26

III The Prince's Chamber

The wide ranging plans for the Royal Gallery were never achieved: but in the smaller adjoining apartment, the Prince's Chamber, a most elaborate and complex scheme was realised. The Chamber is a lofty apartment, the last stage but one in the royal procession at the opening of parliament, and one which also forms an ante-room to the House of Lords used daily by Members of the House. It takes its name from an earlier ante-room (originally the 13th century chapel built for Eleanor of Castile) which occupied a similar position in the old palace.

When they came to consider how best to decorate this Chamber, the Royal Commissioners consciously followed what their secretary, Sir Charles Eastlake, had called 'a character of harmony and unity'. Each part of the Palace was to express 'some specific idea', and in choosing these ideas 'the especial destination of each portion of the building should be attended to'. The idea selected was that of the glories of the Tudor monarchy, which had revived the nation's fortunes after the Wars of the Roses. The upper panels of the 'Royal Antechamber' (as the Commissioners called it) were to be covered with copies of the famous Spanish Armada tapestry described above, which were destroyed in the 1834 fire. The middle compartments were to be filled with

'portraits relating to the Tudor family'. Below these, twelve panels 'in carved work' were to illustrate selected dramatic episodes of Tudor history. And over all, a massive sculpture of the ruling Queen, Victoria, was to preside.

Most of these plans were put into effect, and commissions went out for

1 a group of statues by John Gibson showing Queen Victoria supported by the allegorical figures of Justice and Clemency;
2 bas-reliefs by William Theed, illustrating scenes from sixteenth century British history; and
3 above the bas-reliefs, portraits of Tudor monarchs, wives and other relations, executed, in imitation of surviving contemporary likenesses, by Richard Burchett and his pupils.

These Tudor portraits are of special interest because they were supposed to be taken from authentic sources. The search for those sources was one of the contributory causes of the foundation of the National Portrait Gallery in 1856.

As one of the parts of the Palace through which Queen Victoria had to pass to reach the Lords Chamber, it was important that the Prince's Chamber should be decorated as quickly as possible. As a result, the fireplaces, wainscotting and stained glass were all completed in 1847. The east and west ends each had three windows, whose glass contained in each light the rose of England, thistle of Scotland and shamrock of Ireland, bordered by a narrow fillet of roses. (This was destroyed in the recent war and is now replaced by royal personal armorial glass.) Below the windows runs a frieze of carved oak decorated with the English oak leaf and acorn, and with shields blazoned and gilded with the arms of the Sovereigns of England since the Norman Conquest.

The doorway on the south side leading into the Royal Gallery is heavily decorated: four shields with the arms of England, Ireland and Wales alternate with roses in the intervals of the moulding. The same shields are echoed in stencilled compartments of the ceiling. Another frequent motif is the English lion, which appears in several shapes: at the head of Pugin's chairs which stand by his octagonal tables, on the shields of the fire dogs, and, alternating with the Royal monogram (VR, Victoria Regina), on the red and blue encaustic tiles in the fire places. In the arch over each fireplace are shields with the mottos of England, Scotland and Ireland – 'Dieu et mon Droit', 'Nemo me Impune Lacessit', and 'Quis Separabit?'.

Once the decoration was completed, the first artist to be commissioned was John Gibson, who had already sculpted a statue of the young Queen (now at Osborne). At the Commissioners' insistence he left Rome, and prepared his work in a small room below the Victoria Tower. Prince Albert realized that the niche allotted to the statue of the Queen was too wide for a single figure and Gibson suggested Wisdom and Justice. Albert changed the suggestion to Justice and Clemency (or Mercy), 'as the Sovereign is a Lady'.

The statues are colossal. The young Queen is eight feet (2·44 m) high and the other figures about seven feet (2·13 m). Gibson wrote of his work: 'I have aimed at the highest style of art in severe simplicity: rich and broad drapery, with correctness of outline throughout the whole. This 'grandiosa maniera' can only be imbibed in Rome'. The statuary group is rich in symbols of the most obvious kind. The Queen herself holds a sceptre and laurel crown, as an indication that she both governs and rewards. (Gibson describes the laurel as 'an emblem of the honour conferred upon intellect and valour'.) Behind the Throne are lions, expressive of British strength and courage, and the footstool is adorned by sea-horses which signify British dominion upon the ocean. Justice stands on the right of the Sovereign with a sword in one hand and balance in the other. Her expression is inflexible and round her neck is hung an image of Truth. On the left of the young Queen stands Clemency, who keeps her sword sheathed and offers an olive branch as a sign of peace. The three panels of the pedestal are decorated. Commerce sits in a central panel surrounded by bales and casks. On the left is Science, in this case shown by a youth pondering over volumes of Euclid and Newton, and on the right is a figure denoting Technological Progress. In the background appear a steam engine, a telegraph wire, 'and other useful objects'. (See figure xxvii).

Justice and Mercy, as they are now known, have always been controversial figures. As early as 1856, a leader in *The Builder* complained that the group was 'altogether out of place ... the chamber is dwarfed and its congruity is destroyed'. For twenty years (1955–76) the two flanking figures were banished to storage at Woolwich, during which time part of Justice's scales was lost. That they are now back in the House marks an increasing appreciation of 'one of the greatest pieces of neo-classical sculpture' (Boase).

The sculptor of the bas-reliefs, William Theed the Younger (1804–91) was, like Gibson, *persona grata* with the Prince Consort, who acquired some of his work and gave him various commissions. Queen Victoria continued this royal favour. It was Theed who made the Prince's deathmask for the Queen, as well as the main memorial bust.

The designs for the bronzes were shown at the Royal Academy in the middle 1850s and executed in bronze by Elkingtons. They are three-dimensional versions of history paintings and forceful representations of the scenes they depict, despite their lack of colour, Unlike the royal portraits, however, they display no direct reference to such genuine historical paintings as were available (such as those of the Cloth of Gold). Where practicable the reliefs are set under the relevant portraits – as with Lady Jane Grey; but the positions of the larger plaques are determined by the architectural spacing.

The bas-reliefs, impressive in subject and execution alike, are dominated by a series of full-length royal portraits, reminiscent of paintings devised by Pugin in 1837 for the King's room at Scarisbrick Hall, Lancashire, which Mr Croft-Murray regards as probably the work of Edmund Thomas Parris, history-painter to Queen Adelaide. The Westminster paintings were carried out, under the direction of Richard Burchett of the Royal School of Fine Art at South Kensington and the Government School of Design. by students of the former institution, from 1854 onwards. In 1860 Burchett described to Eastlake with great care the authorities on which he had relied to secure 'a series of true effigies of the personages represented in their habits as they lived' (these are noted below in the appropriate caption). The painting of Henry VII, for example, was based partly on Leemput's copy of Holbein's portrait of that King and partly on the latter's effigy by Torrigiano on his tomb in the Abbey. Similarly the costume in the portrait of Mary I was based on a contemporary portrait belonging to the Society of Antiquaries. As will be seen, later scholarship has shown that not all of Burchett's ascriptions were correct, but the splendour of the general effect is not in doubt. It also reflects great credit on his student-assistants, who, incidentally, included in their number future Academicians like (Sir) Luke Fildes and the portraitist W W Ouless.

The paintings are in oil – it would indeed have been absurd to try to convert to fresco the style of the Tudor portraits on which they are based. A little surface cleaning is all that has ever been applied to them and they must be almost as brilliant today as when Queen Victoria saw them in the 1850s.

References

Port, 263; Walker, ii, 146–150 and iii, 102; T Matthews *The Life of J Gibson, RA* (1911), 107 ff; E Croft-Murray, *Decorative Painting in England (1537–1837)*, vol. ii (1970), 45–46 and plate 69.

27 *Catherine of Aragon pleading*
William Theed, 1855, bronze relief panel, 30 × 32 ins
(76·32 × 81·41 cm)
INSCRIBED W. Theed Sculp. Executed by Elkington, Mason
& Co.
Model exhibited R A 1854
Walker, iii, 102

28 *Raleigh spreading his coat as a carpet for Queen
Elizabeth I*
William Theed, 1855, bronze relief panel, 30 × 31 ins
(76·32 × 78·86 cm)
INSCRIBED as 27, with date.
Model completed 1853 and exhibited R A 1853
Walker, iii, 102

29 *The Death of Sir Philip Sidney*
William Theed, ?1855, bronze relief panel, 30 × 31 ins
(76·32 × 78·86 cm)
No inscription
Model completed July 1852 and exhibited R A 1853
Walker, iii, 102

30 *Sebastian Cabot before Henry VII*
William Theed, 1856, bronze relief panel, 30 × 31 ins
(76·32 × 78·86 cm)
INSCRIBED as 27, with date
Model exhibited R A 1854
Walker, iii, 102

31 *Edward VI granting a charter to Christ's Hospital*
William Theed, ?1855, bronze relief panel, 30 × 32 ins
(76·32 × 81·41 cm)
No inscription
Model completed 1853
Walker, iii, 102

32 *Lady Jane Grey at her studies*
William Theed, 1855, bronze relief panel, 30 × 31 ins
(76·32 × 78·86 cm)
INSCRIBED as 27, with date
Model completed in 1853
Walker, iii, 102

33 *The Field of the Cloth of Gold*
William Theed, ?1855, bronze relief panel,
30 × 89 ins (76·32 × 226·42 cm)
No inscription
Walker, iii, 102

34 *The Visit of the Emperor Charles V to King
Henry VIII*
William Theed, ?1855, bronze relief panel,

30 × 89 ins (76·32 × 226·42 cm)
No inscription
Walker, iii, 102

35 *Queen Elizabeth I knighting Drake*
William Theed, ?1855, bronze relief panel,
30 × 76 ins (76·32 × 193·34 cm)
INSCRIBED as 27
Walker, iii, 102

36 *The escape of Mary, Queen of Scots*
William Theed, ?1855, bronze relief panel,
30 × 76 ins (76·32 × 193·34 cm)
INSCRIBED as 27
Model completed 1853 and exhibited R A 1854
Walker, iii, 102

37 *Mary Queen of Scots looking back on France*
William Theed, 1855, bronze relief panel, 30 × 30 ins
(76·32 × 76·32 cm)
INSCRIBED as 27, with date
Model completed 1853, exhibited R A 1853
Walker, iii, 102

38 *The Murder of Rizzio*
William Theed, ?1856, bronze relief panel, 30 × 32 ins
(76·32 × 81·41 cm)
No inscription
Model exhibited R A 1856
Walker, iii, 102

HENRY VII   ELIZTH OF YORK   A^R P^E WALES   K OF ARAGON

The Sixteenth Century Portraits in the Prince's Chamber

The portraits, nos 39–68, were executed by Richard Burchett with the assistance of his pupils at the Royal School of Art, South Kensington in the years between 1854 and 1860. They were painted in oil on panel. They were based on the best available authorities, the most important of which are noted below in each instance. They are of two standard dimensions, the larger (those on the east and west panels) each 6 ft × 3 ft (183·17 × 91·58 cm) and the smaller (those on the north and south panels) 6 ft × 2ft 7 ins (183·17 × 78·86 cm). For further information on the series see Walker, ii, 146–150. The authorities noted are those on which Burchett depended as given by him in a letter of 14 February 1860 to Sir Charles Eastlake, modified by amendments made by Mr Walker, *op.cit.* and Mr Charlton.

NORTH-EAST PANEL

39 *King Henry VII (1457–1509)*
Authority, the head is derived from the bronze effigy by Torrigiano on the tomb in Westminster Abbey; the rest from a wall-painting by Holbein of Henry VII and his family painted in 1537 in the Privy Chamber in Whitehall Palace, destroyed in a fire, 1697–8. A copy by Rémy van Leemput (of 1667) survived. (E Croft-Murray, *Decorative Painting in England, 1537–1837*, i (1962), 19–20, 22.)

40 *Queen Elizabeth of York (1465–1503)*
Authorities, her tomb at Westminster Abbey and Van Leemput as for No 39.

41 *Arthur, Prince of Wales (1486-1502), eldest son of King Henry VII*
Authority, probably a picture once reputed to be of Henry VII's children when young by Mabuse, a copy of which is at Hampton Court (in fact the portraits are of the children of King Christian of Denmark).

42 *Queen Katherine of Aragon (1485–1536), first wife of King Henry VIII*
Authority, a contemporary miniature in the possession of the Duke of Buccleuch.

EAST PANEL
43 *King Henry VIII (1491–1547)*
Authority, a half-length by Holbein at Windsor Castle, and other portraits.

44 *Queen Anne Boleyn (1507–1536), second wife of King Henry VIII*
Authority, in fact a portrait (copy) of another Anne, Queen of Hungary (1503–1547).

45 *Queen Jane Seymour (1509–1537), third wife of King Henry VIII*
Authority, various portraits, principally the family group noted in no 41 (from which in particular the costume and dog were derived).

46 *Queen Anne of Cleves (1515–1557), fourth wife of King Henry VIII*
Authority, principally an engraving by W Hollar of a portrait now in the Louvre.

47 *Queen Katherine Howard (d 1542), fifth wife of King Henry VIII*
Authority, a miniature in the possession of the Duke of Buccleuch, another version of which is in the Royal Collection.

48 *Queen Katherine Parr (1512–1548), sixth wife of King Henry VIII*
Authority, a portrait now identified as being of Lady Jane Grey, once owned by the Earls of Denbigh, sold at Christies on 1 July 1938 and acquired by the National Portrait Gallery in 1965.

HENRY VIII · · K of ARAGON

49 *King Henry VIII*
(see also no 43).

50 *Queen Catherine of Aragon*
(see also no 42).

(see also no 43).

SOUTH-EAST PANEL
51 *King Edward VI (1537–1553)*
Authority, the portrait by Holbein at Windsor Castle, with the legs only added.

52 *Queen Mary I (1516–1558)*
Authority, portraits by Lucas de Heere, one of which is in the collection of the Society of Antiquaries.

53 *King Philip, II of Spain, I of England (1527–1598)*
Authority, portrait, said to be by Titian, previously in the collection of Earl Stanhope.

54 *Queen Elizabeth I (1553–1603)*
Authority, 'Queen Elizabeth confounding Juno, Minerva and Venus' by Hans Eworth, at Hampton Court.

WEST PANEL

55 *Lady Jane Grey (Lady Jane Dudley, wife of Lord Guildford Dudley) 1537–1554), proclaimed Queen 1553, executed 1554.*
Authority, portrait of an uncrowned Flemish Lady by the Maitre des Femmes à mi-corps (Walker, ii, 149), mistaken by Burchett to be of Lady Jane.

56 *Lord Guildford Dudley (d 1554), fourth son of John, Duke of Northumberland, husband of Lady Jane (Grey).*
Authority, head only from what may be a *c* 1580–90 portrait of an unidentified man.

57 *King James IV of Scotland (1473–1513), husband of Margaret, the daughter of King Henry VII.*

Authorities, 'Several scarce old engravings, the head only copied' (Burchett, in Walker, ii, 149).

58 *The Princess Margaret, Queen Margaret of Scotland (1489–1541), daughter of King Henry VII, wife of King James IV.*
Authority, what is now considered to be a portrait of Madame de Canaples in the National Gallery of Scotland.

59 *Archibald Douglas, Earl of Angus (d 1557), second husband of Queen Margaret of Scotland.*
Authority, head derived from a portrait at Windsor Castle.

60 *King James V of Scotland (1512–1542), son of King James IV and Queen Margaret, father of Mary Queen of Scots.*
Authority, none given by Burchett or Walker.

SOUTH-WEST PANEL

61 *King Louis XII of France (1462–1515), first husband of Princess Mary, the daughter of King Henry VII.*
Authority, 'A very fine missal illuminating the property of Lord Taunton . . . . . representing him at prayer' (Burchett, Walker, ii, 148).

62 *Princess Mary (1496–1533), subsequently Queen of King Louis XII of France, daughter of King Henry VII.*
Authority, none given (Walker, ii, 148).

63 *Charles Brandon, 1st Duke of Suffolk (d 1545), second husband of Princess Mary, daughter of King Henry VII.*
Authority, portrait to waist in the Duke of Bedford's collection (Walker, ii, 148).

64 *Frances, Marchioness of Dorset (1517–1559), daughter of Charles Brandon and Princess Mary, nos 62, 63.*
Authority, portrait probably by Hans Eworth, with costume details from tomb in Westminster Abbey (Walker, ii, 148).

Mᴿˢ ᴼᶠ GUISE   MARY SCOTS   FRANCIS II   Lᴰ DARNLEY

NORTH-WEST PANEL

65 *Mary of Guise (1515–1560), Queen of Scotland, wife of King James V, mother of Mary, Queen of Scots.*
Authority, contemporary portrait in the collection of the Duke of Devonshire.

66 *Mary, Queen of Scots (1542–1587), daughter of King James V.*
Authority, a miniature, now ascribed to François Clouet, in the Royal Collection, and other portraits (cf Walker, ii, 150).

67 *King Francis II of France (1544–1560), husband of Mary, Queen of Scots.*
Authority, portrait, head only, by Janet at Hampton Court.

68 *Henry, Lord Darnley (1545–1567), husband of Mary, Queen of Scots.*
Authorities, 'Portraits, said to be by Lucas de Heere, in the collection at Hampton Court, and an old engraving by Elstrake' (Burchett, Walker, ii, 150).

IV The House of Lords Chamber

The Chamber of the House of Lords is more properly known as the 'Parliament Chamber' for it is here that the whole Parliament assembles – nowadays mainly on the occasion of the State Opening. Then The Queen is seated on her Throne accompanied by members of her family and household; the Lords Spiritual and Temporal sit on the benches, with their 'Assistants', the Judges of the High Court, on woolsacks; and the 'faithful Commons' led by their Speaker stand at the bar of the House. The room was built with this ceremonial and necessarily crowded occasion in mind. It is therefore richly ornamented, and also a good deal larger than is needed for the daily sittings of the Lords; it is 80×45 ft ($24 \cdot 42 \times 13 \cdot 74$ m) as against the Commons Chamber's dimensions of 68 ft $\times$ 45 ft 6 ins ($20 \cdot 72 \times 13 \cdot 87$ m).

The splendour planned for this Chamber early received hostile criticism. On 26th May 1846 Joseph Hume, ever watchful for instances of improper privilege on the part of the unelected House, complained in the House of Commons. The Lords, he said, were receiving special attention in the decoration of the New Palace: why should that House and that Chamber be more richly decorated than was intended for the House of Commons? Peel, the Prime Minister, attempted to allay his suspicions, but undoubtedly they were justified. In the Lords a

degree of priority was given and a level of embellishment attained that was unattempted by Barry and Pugin anywhere else in the Palace.

The difficulties under which both men laboured in the later 1840s were considerable. Barry in London was separated from the workshops of his two chief lieutenants in the decoration, Pugin's (at Ramsgate) and Hardman's (in Birmingham). Much of the business was carried on by correspondence, then – a correspondence from which Barry was all too often diverted by attacks in both Houses and outside them, by a protracted controversy with the cranky ventilating engineer, Dr Reid and by an incessant stream of distinguished visitors, of whom one of the most frequent was the Prince Consort himself, Chairman of the new Fine Arts Commission. Indeed, so persistent were the Prince's attentions that they were noticed by Mr Punch, who in a satirical article of 1847 began his own fresco (fig xvi) and observed with glee 'Prince Albert can hardly be persuaded to quit my *atelier*. Mr Rogers (another Commissioner) disputes with Toby the honour of cleaning my palette ... The Commissioners of the Fine Arts are buzzing around me'.

However, in spite of all these distractions the Chamber was one of the first parts of the New Palace to be completed: by 14th April, 1847. Its dominant feature, the Throne, was Pugin's chef d'oeuvre. Undoubtedly 'closely based upon the Coronation Chair in Westminster Abbey . . . one of the few documented pieces of medieval furniture known in Pugin's day' it set a standard of grandeur with its triple compartments, large dais, elaborate carving and gilding, that made essential similarly rich decoration throughout the Chamber. The result is that whereas 'works of art', that is, frescoes and sculpture, dominate the Royal Gallery and at least hold their own in the Robing Room, in the Chamber they are recessive, frescoes occupying the six arched recesses above the galleries at the north and south ends of the Chamber. The eye is taken rather by the red upholstery of benches and woolsack and the standing brass candlelabra, the linenfold panelling, and the (recent) stained glass windows showing coats of arms of bishops and peers from the centuries between 1360 and 1900. Sir Nikolaus Pevsner has pointed out the importance of the Victorian decoration on the Throne and elsewhere in the Chamber . . . 'an inexhaustible wealth of invention'. He comments that 'One reads so much about the dead and mechanical work of the Victorian craftsmen. It is to these pieces of Pugin's design that one ought to look to appreciate what craftsmen in the 1840s were capable of, if spurred by a fanatic mind'.

It has been hard for the six frescoes to compete with this virtuosity of craftsmanship. As has been described above, the competitions held in 1845 for the fresco painting in the Chamber was even at the time not regarded as having resulted in any great success, and today the Lords Chamber frescoes are praised for their 'unobtrusive tones' rather than their design. The final choice of subjects, however, is not without interest. Here in the principal Parliamentary chamber the artists speak directly to Parliament: in three instances they directly extol virtues which the Victorian age sought in its society: justice, religion and chivalry; in the three other frescoes these virtues are expressed in historical narrative. Henry V as a prince encounters the meaning of justice; King Ethelbert acknowledges religion by baptism into the church; Edward III crystallizes the spirit of chivalry by founding the Order of the Garter and making his son a Knight. Moreover, the history is from the Middle Ages, for by the 1840s poets, historians and divines alike were teaching the country to regard the 'high Middle Ages' not as a dark period of superstition, but as seminal, the historic point at which universities, some of the arts, our national language, and indeed Parliament itself originated. A generation later Bishop Stubbs was to sanctify the concept of the 'Model Parliament' of 1295 but John Lingard had already published his eight volumes extolling medieval achievements (in 1830), and was shortly to issue his fifth edition in 10 volumes (in 1849). The Parliament Chamber frescoes were very much of their age. It is only to be wondered that neither here nor elsewhere in the Palace are there attempts to represent sittings of the medieval Parliament itself. The emphasis throughout pictorially was (except in the 17th century subjects) on national rather than on specifically Parliamentary history.

References

Port, chapters vii and xii; *KW*, vi, 621; *Illustrated London News*, 17th April 1847; Walker, iv, *passim*; N Pevsner, *Cities of London and Westminster* (1957), 460.

69 *The Spirit of Justice*
Daniel Maclise, 1849, fresco, 16 ft 4½ ins × 9 ft 4 ins
(5 × 2·85 m) (North Gallery)
Walker, iv, 65 (see also O'Driscoll, 104–5 and
Daniel Maclise, (Arts Council, 1972). 87–88)

70 *Prince Henry acknowledging the authority of Chief Justice Gascoyne*
C W Cope, 1849, fresco on plaster, 16 ft $4\frac{1}{2}$ ins × 9 ft $4\frac{1}{2}$ ins
(5 × 2·86 m) (South Gallery)
Walker, iv, 14–15

71 *The Spirit of Chivalry*
Daniel Maclise, 1847, fresco, 16 ft 4½ ins × 9 ft 4½ ins
(5 × 2·86 m) (North Gallery)
Walker, iv, 61–2; *Daniel Maclise*, 84–87

72 *Edward III conferring the Order of the Garter on the Black Prince*
C W Cope, 1848, fresco on plaster, 16 ft 4½ ins × 9 ft 4½ ins (5 × 2·86 m) (South Gallery)
Walker, iv, 10–13

73 *The Spirit of Religion*
J C Horsley, 1847, fresco on plaster (repainted in
tempera, see p 41 above), 16 ft 4½ ins × 9 ft 4½ ins
(5 × 2·86 m) (North Gallery)
Walker, iv, 52–53

74 *The Baptism of King Ethelbert*
William Dyce, 1846, fresco, 16 ft 4$\frac{1}{2}$ ins × 9 ft 4$\frac{1}{2}$ ins
(5 × 2·86 m) (South Gallery)
Walker, iv, 28–29

V The Peers' Corridor

A vaulted passage, known as the Peers' Corridor, leads from the bronze, red and gold of the Peers' Lobby into the high-arching Central Lobby of the New Palace of Westminster. More obviously, perhaps, than the grander splendours of the royal apartments this corridor reminds its viewers that the New Palace was a building first conceived as essentially utilitarian in character.

Down the Peers' Corridor Messengers, Clerks and Members of both Houses have passed hourly and through it have approached witnesses to committees, guests of peers and members of the public (whose interest in parliamentary proceedings had for the first time been recognised as legitimate by the construction of permanent Strangers' Galleries in both the new Chambers). The Corridor in particular links the two Chambers and it is to be noted that they lie along a single axis. It is appropriate that its decoration – one of the focal sequences of works of art in the Palace – should reflect the struggles by which national liberties had been established, and after the more general themes of the previous apartments, should approach closely the history of Parliament itself. In the Peers' Corridor, for the first time, Parliament itself enters the historical canvas, and Parliament and the Crown are explicit protagonists of some of the subjects chosen for its walls.

No subjects were more popular for Victorian narrative painters than Charles I, Oliver Cromwell and the struggles of Cavalier and Roundhead. Few afforded more opportunity for romantic incident, as Walter Scott, Balzac, Hugo, Bellini and the young Robert Browning had already discovered. But the scenes chosen for the walls of a Parliamentary corridor were not just individual dramatic episodes of the Stuart period, but part of a deliberate and balanced plan. In the words of the Commissioners,

'... the corridors which join the two Houses might properly be decorated with paintings illustrative of that great contest which commenced with the meeting of the Long Parliament and terminated in 1689. It will be seen that the subjects have been selected on the principle of parallelism, and that an attempt has been made to do justice to the heroic virtues which were displayed on both sides'.

No one was better qualified to make this selection than the Committee appointed, for it included, as has been seen, Lord John Russell, successor and historian of one of the earliest Whig families, Henry Hallam whose *Constitutional History of England* (1827) was already a standard work and Thomas Babington Macaulay, whose own history had yet to appear but whose knowledge of the minutest incidents of British history was unrivalled. The scenes they chose were in closely paralleled pairs:

against a picture of Charles I erecting his standard at Nottingham was to be shown Speaker Lenthall asserting the privileges of the Commons against the King; opposite the defence of Basing House by the Cavaliers, the train bands of London setting out to raise the siege of Gloucester. Oxford Fellows expelled from their colleges by the Puritans were to be set against a Puritan family leaving for New England; and the series was to end with reminders of two of the most famous 17th century executions – the burial of Charles I, and the parting of Lord Russell from his wife in the Tower of London.

To fulfil the Commission's recommendation, C W Cope was chosen, one of the prizewinners in the first competition of 1843 with his *The First Trial by Jury*. Cope had already completed two of the large panels in the Lords Chamber – Prince Henry, and the institution of the Garter – and had illustrated a scene of Griselda from Chaucer's *Clerk's Tale* in the Upper Waiting Hall of the House of Commons in 1849. In 1853 he was commissioned to paint the series at £500 for the first picture and £450 for the rest. Cope began with a version in oil of *A Puritan Family Leaving for New England,* which he chose to misinterpret as *The Departure of the Mayflower* (an incident which took place twenty years before the outbreak of the Civil War). The design was satisfactory, but the medium was not – 'the gloss of surface, necessarily characteristic of painting in oil, was detrimental'. Cope changed for his first four paintings to fresco, but by 1860 his earlier frescoes in the Upper Waiting Hall were utterly dilapidated. He switched for the last four to

waterglass, and the price awarded for each went up to £700. By 1867 the complete series was installed in the Peers' Corridor.

Inaccurate and anachronistic in much of their detail (none more so than the *Mayflower* scene), Cope's Stuart frescoes are nevertheless a peculiar triumph. They not only celebrate the intensity of Victorian interest in the Stuart period, and represent vividly the 19th century idea of the artist as antiquarian; they also confirm the conviction of the Victorian Englishman that his political good-fortune was unrivalled. The struggles shown in Cope's Peers' Corridor frescoes had established the basic principles of the constitution – the prevention of arbitrary rule by the monarch; the rights of both Houses of Parliament to freedom of speech; and the determination of minorities of the population to establish their right to freedom of religious worship. A Victorian walking down the Peers' Corridor would feel no unease at the violent struggles portrayed on either side: for these scenes, in the words of Roy Strong, 'reflected battles for basic liberties won long ago, and inspired a calm confidence in the destiny of this island and its ideal parliamentary democracy'. As Hallam, who had helped to choose them, had written,

'No unbiased observer, who derives pleasure from the welfare of his species, can fail to consider the long and uninterruptedly increasing prosperity of England as the most beautiful phenomenon in the history of mankind'.

References

Strong, 136–145; Port, 275; Seventh Report of the Royal Commission on the Fine Arts, PP 1847 (862), xxxiii App. 1: *Report of the Committee appointed to select Subjects in Painting and Sculpture.*

75 *Lord Russell taking leave of his wife before going to his execution for complicity in the Rye House Plot*
C W Cope, 1859, fresco, 7 ft 2½ ins × 9 ft 4½ ins (2·20 × 2·86 m)

INSCRIBED, C W Cope Oct 12 1859
Walker, iv, 18 (see also, for nos 77–84, Cope, chapter viii and *passim*)
See p 39 for details concerning the restoration of nos 77–84.

76 *The embarkation of the Pilgrim Fathers for*
New England in 1620
C W Cope, 1856, fresco, 7 ft $2\frac{1}{2}$ ins × 9 ft $4\frac{1}{2}$ ins
(2·20 × 2·86 m)
INSCRIBED, C W Cope 1856
Walker, iv, 16

77 *The Setting out of the Train Bands from London to raise the Siege of Gloucester, 1643*
C W Cope, 1865, waterglass painting,
7 ft 2½ ins × 9 ft 4½ ins (2·20 × 2·86 m)
INSCRIBED, Waterglass C W Cope 1865
Walker, iv, 22

78 *Speaker Lenthall asserting the privileges of the House of Commons when King Charles I came to arrest the Five Members, 1642*
C W Cope, 1866, waterglass painting,

7 ft 2½ ins × 9 ft 4½ ins (2·20 × 2·86 m)
INSCRIBED [on document], 1866 C W Cope in Water Glass [on the step] C W Cope 1866
Walker, iv, 23

79 *King Charles I raising his standard at Nottingham, 1642*

C W Cope, 1861, fresco, 7 ft 2½ ins × 9 ft 4½ ins
(2·20 × 2·86 m)

INSCRIBED, C W Cope, Augt 4 1861 [and] CWC
1861

Walker, iv, 19

80 *The expulsion of the Fellows of a College at*
Oxford for refusing to sign the Covenant
C W Cope, 1865, waterglass painting,
7 ft 2½ ins × 9 ft 4½ ins (2·20 × 2·86 m)
INSCRIBED [on the inkpot], C W Cope 1865
Walker, iv, 21

81 *Basing House defended by the Cavaliers against the Parliamentary Army, 1645*
C W Cope, 1862, waterglass painting,
7 ft $2\frac{1}{2}$ ins × 9 ft $4\frac{1}{2}$ ins (2·20 × 2·86 m)

INSCRIBED [in swordblade], CWC–1862 [also]
C W Cope 1862
Walker, iv, 20

82 *The burial of King Charles I at Windsor*
C W Cope, 1857, fresco, 7 ft 2½ ins × 9 ft 4½ ins
(2·20 × 2·86 m)
No inscription
Walker, iv, 17

VI Sculpture in the Norman Porch

The sculpture in relief in the House of Lords has already been described and illustrated: the oak bas-reliefs of H H Armstead in the Royal Robing Room and the bronze reliefs by William Theed in the Princes' Chamber – together with the freestanding group by John Gibson of Queen Victoria, Justice and Mercy in the same Chamber. There remains a group of busts resulting from loan, gift and purchase which decorate the House of Lords. Certain of these are in the Library and in Corridors off the main line of route. The main part of the collection is, however, placed at the beginning of the route in the vaulted space conceived of from the beginning as a display area with a high degree of decoration. It starts at the head of the Royal Staircase, an uninterrupted flight of 25 steps with 5-inch (12·72 cm) rises and 16-inch (40·7 cm) treads designed for ease of mounting. Since 1845 this area has been known as the 'Norman Porch' because of a decision by the Fine Arts Commissioners on 25th April, 1845

'that the principal Landing-place should contain the statues of the Sovereigns from William the Conqueror to Edward IV'.

There is in fact nothing remotely Norman about the Porch as it was finally constructed. The staircase leading up to the Porch derived heavily from Sir John Soane's designs for a Scala Regia in the 1820s. On the landing itself, from a floor inlaid with Devonshire and Irish marble and encaustic tiles, a clustered central pillar rises to meet the intersection of four small Gothic vaults. A small circular light (of glass to the design of Pugin's son-in-law J H Powell) has been set into the centre of each vault, the rest of whose ceilings are thickly crowded with painted stone bosses, showing the personal and heraldic emblems of the English monarchs – griffins, wyverns, pelicans and swans are among the winged creatures who have come to roost there. Both the bosses and the ornate carved and gilded work around the doors of the Queen's and the Prince's Robing Rooms were completed by the younger Barry in the 1860s.

It is hard to say quite why the sculptures ordered in 1845 for the Norman Porch were not undertaken. Charles Barry was responsible for sculpture *as architectural decoration,* and under his management and that of John Thomas (the Gloucestershire mason who became Superintendent of stone carving at the Palace) the series of saints and kings decorating the whole exterior was completed at great speed. The Fine Arts Commission, with whom rested responsibility for what was termed *'insulated'* (i.e. freestanding) sculpture, was much less efficient. The whole subject was covered in principle in an early Report (their Fourth, of 1845). The Magna Carta barons and prelates for the Parliament

Chamber were chosen and modelled, and the first three in a series of parliamentary orators (now in St Stephens Hall) were also commissioned. But of the 121 names on the 'general list of distinguished persons ... to whose memory statues might with propriety be erected', only ten found their way into stone; and of the complete run of English monarchs, only the statues now in the Central Lobby were completed to plan. (The gilded series by Birnie Philip in the Royal Gallery was the result of a later decision, by Edward Barry.) It was clear that the increasing preoccupations of the key Commissioners, Prince Albert and Sir Robert Peel, and their Secretary Charles Eastlake, deprived the Government of the impetus necessary to press, and pay, for the completion of the sculptural programme.

A later Report of the Commissioners (the Seventh, of 1847), if implemented, would have added still more to the decoration of the Norman Porch. The Committee appointed by the Commissioners proposed two sea-side subjects to fill the wall panels, each 18 ft 2 ins (5·54 m) (at the point of the arch) by 10 ft 10 ins (3·31 m). These were to be *Canute reproving his Courtiers* and *Queen Elizabeth on the sea-side after the defeat of the Spanish Armada*. In the event, neither even reached the cartoon stage.

The Norman Porch remained for almost a century as the younger Barry had left it when his commission was terminated in 1870 by what was to be described in the Commons as 'a letter which no gentleman would send to his butler'. The present completion of empty pedestals by the addition of busts of peers who were Prime Ministers was the suggestion of the Lord Great Chamberlain in 1963. Traditionally the Lord Great Chamberlain is responsible to the Monarch for Her Majesty's Palace of Westminster, and even after 1965, when the Queen vested the responsibility for Lords and Commons parts of the Palace with the two Speakers, the Lord Great Chamberlain (then the 5th Marquess of Cholmondeley) retained responsibility for the Royal Apartments, within which the Norman Porch lies.

The series of busts gathered as a result of his initiative form a coherent collection. Some were lent by the National Portrait Gallery; one was presented by the Duke of Wellington and two by the President of the Royal Society of British Artists, the portraitist Edward Halliday; and the Lord Great Chamberlain himself presented several and commissioned copies of others, to complete the series. As in the Victorian Palace, the quality of work is variable – the series includes an example of Nollekens' work, together with two further casts after him, and also busts by Joseph Wilton (of the Earl of Chatham) and E H Baily (of the Duke of Wellington). But there can be no doubt that Lord Cholmondeley's inspiration brought to completion, for the Norman Porch, the 'great idea' which had animated Charles Barry in his early evidence to the Royal Commission:

'Sculpture without, sculpture, painting and stained glass within, are to preserve the memorials of the past and declare the date and object of the building'.

References

Port, 232–245; PP 1845 (671), xxvii, Fourth Report of the Royal Commission on the Fine Arts, App. 1 and 4, and 1847 (862), xxxiv, App. 1; Walker, supplements i and ii; 3 Parl. Deb, cci, 717.

NOTE:
The busts are, except where noted, carved in marble; in the captions the name of the sculptor is given (where known), together with the date, height of the bust, and the appropriate reference to the Walker catalogue.

83 *William Pitt, 1st Earl of Chatham (1708–1778), Prime Minister 1766–68*
Joseph Wilton, *post* 1780, 29 ins (73·77 cm)
INSCRIBED Wm Pitt, Earl of Chatham
Walker, supplement i, 4

84 *Charles Watson-Wentworth, 2nd Marquess of Rockingham (1738–82), Prime Minister 1765–6, 1782*
Joseph Nollekens, *c* 1776, 29 ins (73·77 cm)
INSCRIBED Nollekens Ft
Walker, supplement ii, 2

85 *William Wyndham Grenville, Lord Grenville (1759–1834), Prime Minister 1806–7*
Copy after Nollekens, 27 ins (68·69 cm)
INSCRIBED 71 (Crown) Nollekens Ft 1810

86 *Robert Banks Jenkinson, 2nd Earl of Liverpool (1770–1828), Prime Minister 1812–27*
Copy after Nollekens, 27 ins (68·69 cm)
INSCRIBED 59 (Crown) Nollekens F 1816

83

84

85

86

87 *Arthur Wellesley, 1st Duke of Wellington (1769–1852), Prime Minister 1828–30*
Edward Hodges Baily, *c* 1830, 31 ins (78·86 cm)
SIGNED E H Baily, RA sculpt
Walker, supplement i, 25

88 *Charles Grey, 2nd Earl Grey (1764–1845), Prime Minister 1830–34*
Thomas Campbell, 1827, 27 ins (68·69 cm)
INSCRIBED, THOMAS CAMPBELL SCULPT. 1827

89 *William Lamb, 2nd Viscount Melbourne (1779–1848), Prime Minister 1834, 1835–41*
Copy after John Francis by the British Museum, $29\frac{1}{2}$ ins (75·04 cm)

90 *John Russell, 1st Earl Russell (1792–1878), Prime Minister 1846–52, 1865–6*
John Francis, 1832, $27\frac{1}{2}$ ins (69·96 cm)
INSCRIBED LORD JOHN RUSSELL, 1832
Walker, supplement i, 21

87

88

89

90

91 *Edward Stanley, 14th Earl of Derby*
(1799–1869), Prime Minister 1852, 1858–9,
1866–8
Feodora, Countess Gleichen, 1892, 32 ins
(81·41 cm)
SIGNED F G sculpt 1892
Walker, supplement i, 7

92 *George Hamilton-Gordon, 4th Earl of*
Aberdeen (1784–1860), Prime Minister 1852–5
Copy after Matthew Noble made by V
d'Alessandro, 1964, 32 ins (81·41 ins)
Walker, supplement i, 1

91

92

93 *Benjamin Disraeli, Earl of Beaconsfield*
(1804–1881), Prime Minister 1868, 1874–80
Victor, Count Gleichen, 1880, 32 ins (81·41 cm)
SIGNED G 1880
Walker, supplement i, 3

94 *Archibald Philip Primrose, 5th Earl of*
Rosebery (1847–1929), Prime Minister, 1894–95
Copy after Sir Joseph Boehm, by V
d'Alessandro, 1963, 27 ins (68·69 cm)
Walker, supplement i, 20

93

94

Index of Persons